Carr, Crawley

Discount Sheet to Price List of 1878

Of the Philadelphia Hardware and Malleable Iron Works

Carr, Crawley

Discount Sheet to Price List of 1878

Of the Philadelphia Hardware and Malleable Iron Works

ISBN/EAN: 9783337182397

Printed in Europe, USA, Canada, Australia, Japan

Cover: Foto ©ninafisch / pixelio.de

More available books at **www.hansebooks.com**

DISCOUNT SHEET

to

PRICE LIST OF 1878,

of the

PHILADELPHIA HARDWARE

and

MALLEABLE IRON WORKS.

CARR, CRAWLEY & DEVLIN.

Philadelphia, Sept. 25, 1878.

10 and 10 per cent. off of all ~~Wrought-Iron Stove-Bolts~~

TERMS CASH.

Bills remaining unpaid after the first customary thirty days' average, will be drawn sight, with three days' notice.

Prices subject to change without notice.

PAGE		DISCOUNT PER CENT.
2—2½	Bronze-Metal Butts, No. 105, 106....................	65
3	Bronzed Butts, No. 95..............................	65
3	" " 100................................	65
4	Loose-Pin Panel Butts, No. 15........................	75
5	Acorn Butts, Loose Pin, No. 20......................	70
5	" " 25......................	75
5	" " 30......................	70
6	Narrow Fast Cast Butts, No. 35......................	60
7	" Loose " 40......................	75
8	Broad Fast " 45.......................	65
9	Broad Loose " 50......................	75
10	Mayer's Hinges, No. 55............................	75
11	Parliament " 60............................	65
12	Narrow Fast Cast Butts, Drilled, No. 65.............	55
13	" Loose " " 70............	72½
14	Broad Fast " " 75............	60
15	Broad Loose " " 80............	72½
16	Mayer's Hinges, " 85............	72½
17	Parliament Hinges, " 90............	62½
18	Wrought Iron Inside Blind Hinges, pol., No. 110	40
18	" " " bronzed. 110	60
18	" Narrow, Fast Butts..............115	45
18	" " " bronzed...115	55
19	" Back Flaps......................120	40
19	" Table Hinges....................125	40
19	" Back Flaps......................130	40
20—21	Lull & Porter's Patent Hinges......................	70
21	Gate Hinges..	65
22	Gate Latches.......................................	65
23	Porch Post-Supporters..............................	70
24	Barn-Door Hangers, No. 4...........................	55
25	" " " 2...........................	55
26	" " " 1...........................	35
27	" " " 5...........................	55
28	" " " 3...........................	35
29	" " " 6...........................	35
30	" Rollers......................................	45
30	" Rail...	70
31	Bell Pulleys..	55
32—39	Frame Pulleys......................................	55

40—50	Axle Pulleys	55
51—53	Screw Pulleys	50
54	Side Pulleys	50
55	Upright Pulleys	50
55	Dumb Waiter Pulleys	50
	Awning Pulleys, single (set is lid) 2 in., $1 30 p. doz.	40
	" double " 2 in., $2 10 "	40
56	Clothes-Line Pulleys	40
57	Sliding-Door Sheaves	25
57	" Rail	40
58—59	Chain Door-Fasteners	40
60	Barrel, Tower, and Shutter Bolts	55
61	Shutter Bolts, No. 20	57½
61	" 24	55
61	" 25	45
61	Spring Bolts	40
62	Necked "	30
62	Barrel "	55
62	Square Spring Bolts	55
63	Bottom Bolts	55
64	Spring Bolts	50
64	Staples for Bolts	50
65	Chain Bolts	40
66	Thumb Latches	40
66	" Extra	20
66	Case Latches	65
67	Drop Latches	60
68—69	Store Door Latches	40
70	"	40
71	Barn Door Latches	40
71	Safety Shutter Lowers	25
72—74	Shutter Stays	60
72	Shutter Stay Rosettes	20
75	Inside and Outside Shutter Fasteners	30
75	Inside Shutter-Fasteners	45
75	Shutter Hooks	25
76—77	Wardrobe Hooks	55
78—83	Hat & Coat Hooks, No. 81, $3 50. No. 85, $3 80.	55
83	Gum Spring Hooks	20
84	School-House Hooks	45
85	Head-Board Hooks and Eyes	33½

86—87	Harness Hooks	45
88—89	Ceiling Hooks	50
90—93	Clothes-Line Hooks	50
93—94	Bird Cage Hooks	50
95	Hat-Rack Plates and Hooks	55
96	Lamp Hooks	55
96	Picture Hooks	40
96	Awning Hooks	40
97	Flush Chest Handles	60
97	Wrought Chest Handles	60
98—99	Surface " No. 1872, $3 85	60
100—103	Drawer Pulls	45
104—105	Cupboard Catches	25
104	French Window Catches	25
106—107	Sash Fasteners	40
108	Cupboard Knobs	25
108	Shutter Knobs	25
109	Shutter Bars	33¼
110	Sash Fasteners	20
110	Sash Props	20
111	Sash Lifts	30
112	Stubs and Plates	55
112	Transom Plates	55
112	Shutter Lifts	40
113	Shutter Screws	40
113	Sash Rollers	40
113	Chest Rollers, Malleable Iron, $2 50	25
114	Fence Staples	40
114	Hinge Hasps	30
115	Saw Rods	40
115	Knockers	25
116	Door Buttons	35
116	" on Plates	50
116	Ventilators	25
117	Stay Nails	25
117	Plumb Bobs	40
117	Sheave Wheels	33¼
118	Drawer Pulls	45
118	Door Pulls	25
118	Table-Leaf Supports	50

119	Cloth Clamps	40
119	Quilting Frame Clamps	40
120	Oar Locks	25
121	Rudder Braces	25
122	Cleats	33⅓
123	Tackle Blocks	33⅓
124	Thimbles	25
124	Awning-Frame Plates	33⅓
125	Hatch Rope Eyes	25
125	Rings	33⅓
126	Plate Casters, with Iron or Brass Wheels	50
126	" " Wood Wheels	55
126	" " Porcelain Wheels	55
126	Piano Casters	40
127	Socket Casters	45
127	French Casters	50
128	Bed Casters, with Iron Wheels	50
128	" " Wood Wheels	55
128	" " Porcelain Wheels	55
128	" Globe Wheel	40
129	Bracket Casters	45
129	Sewing Machine Casters	40
130	Box Casters	40
130	Truck Wheels	50
130	Bed Keys	30
131—132	Bedstead Fasteners	40
132	Fire Detectors	30
132	Letter Box Plates	25
132½—133	Tobacco Cutters,	40
134—135	Shade Brackets	66⅔
136—137	Roller Ends, No. 5, $7 00	66⅔
137	Shade Cord Holders	66⅔
138	Shade Racks	66⅔
139	Soap Cups	20
139	Spittoons	30
140—141	Foot Scrapers, No. 2, Japanned, 85 cts	40
142	Grindstone Fixtures	66⅔
143	Friction Rollers	30
143	Garden Hoes	40
143	Potato Hoes	40

143	Garden Rakes	40
144	Gridirons	20
144	Cork Pressers	25
145	Sad-Iron Stands	40
145	Coffee Pot Stands	40
146—147	Lemon Squeezers	33½
148	Boot Jacks	50
148	Foot Rests	20
149	Dumb Bells	80
140	Quoits	30
149	Lathe Carriers	25
150	Well Wheels	50
150	Melting Ladles	80
151	Hay Fork Pulleys	50
152	Ox Balls	10
153	Umbrella Stands	30
154	Druggists' Brackets	40
155	Brackets [Current No. 170 to 8x8 in.]	40
156—157	"	55
158—160	"	85
161	"	35
162	Rings	5
162	Buckles	5
163	Shoe Buckles	5
163	Skate "	5
163	Barrel Roller Buckles	5
164—165	Harness Buckles	5
165	Barrel Roller Buckles, XX	5
166	Malleable Roller Buckles	5
167	" Barrel Roller Buckles	5
168	Bennble Buckles	5
169	" Combination Loop Buckles	5
170	Horse Shoe Trace Buckles	5
170	Barrel Roller Trace Buckles	5
171	Philadelphia " "	5
171	Port Bits	5
172	Ring "	5
172	Snaffle "	5
173—175	Port "	5
176	Rein Swivels	5
177	Bolt Hooks	5
177	Terrets	5
178	Cock Eyes	5

PAGE		DISCOUNT PER CENT.
179	Hame Fasteners	25
179	Breeching Loops	5
180	Halter Bolts	5
180	Trace Loops	5
180	Halter Squares	5
181	Malleable D's	5
181	Halter Triangles	5
181	Stirrups	10
182	Carriage and Coach Hinges	10
183	Carriage Door Dove Tails	10
184	Lazy Back Irons	10
185	Jump Seat Irons (the cut of No. 2 is upside down)	-10
186	Yoke and Swingletree Tips	10
187	Shaft and Pole Tips	10
188	Screw Clamps	15
189—191	Top Props	20
191	Top Prop Nuts and Rivets	20
192	Apron Hooks and Rings	10
192	Chase's Patent Wrenches	10
193—199	Carriage Bands	55
200—232	Malleable Iron Castings, 8 cts lb	0
223	Wrought Iron Felloe Plates, 8 cts lb	0
223	Steel Felloe Plates, 25 cts lb	0
233—241	Malleable Iron Castings, Miscellaneous	0
242	Thornley's Washers	25
242	Cast Iron Washers	0
243	Spring Shackles	10
244—245	Trunk Dove Tails	25
246—248	Trunk Plates, Malleable	25
246	" " Wrought	25
248—249	Trunk Rollers	25
250	Trunk Hinges	25
251	Trunk-Handle Caps	25
252	Trunk Buttons	25
252	Trunk-Handle Loops	25
252	Satchel Plates	25
253	Sauce-Pan Handles	10
253	Damper Handles	10
253	Lid Knobs	10
254	Wrought Iron Ears	40
255	Malleable Iron Ears	0
256	Coal-Hod Handles and Ears	0
257	Dish-Pan Handles	0
258	Stove-Pipe Dampers	33½
258	Coal Shovels	30
259	Roofing Groovers	10
259—264	Castings for Tin and Sheet-Iron Workers	0

CATALOGUE AND PRICE LIST

OF THE

PHILADELPHIA

HARDWARE

AND

MALLEABLE IRON WORKS,

JEFFERSON STREET, FROM EIGHTH TO NINTH,

CARR, CRAWLEY & DEVLIN.

STORES:

307 ARCH STREET, PHILADELPHIA.
118 CHAMBERS STREET, NEW YORK—
              GRAHAM & HAINES, Agents.
5 GERMAN STREET, BALTIMORE,
              S. G. B. COOK & CO., Agents.

INDEX.

A

	PAGE
Acorn Butts, Drilled	5
Apron Hooks and Rings	192
Awning-Frame Plates	124
Awning Hooks	96
Axle Pulleys	40–50

B

Back Flaps, Wrought-Iron	19
Bands, Carriage	193–199
Barn-Door Hangers	24–29
" Latches	71
" Rail	30
" Rollers	30
Bed Casters	128
" Fasteners	131, 132
" Hooks	85
" Keys	130
Bell Pulleys	31
Bird-Cage Hooks	93, 94
Bits, Ring, Port and Snaffle	171–175
Blind Hinges, Inside	18
Blocks, Tackle	123
Bolt Hooks	177
Bolts, Barrel	60
" " Bronzed	62
" Bottom, Bronzed	63
" Chain	65
" Halter	180
" Neck, Wrought	62
" Shutter, Cast	60
" " Wrought	61
" Spring, Cast	64
" " Wrought	61
" " Square, Bronzed	62
" Tower	60
Box Casters	130
Boot Jacks	148

	PAGE
Bracket Casters	129
Brackets, Druggists, Mantel, Shelf	154–161
" Shade	134, 135
Breeching D's	181
" Loops	179
" Rings	162
Bridle Bits	171–175
Bucket Ears	256
Buckles, Harness	164, 165
" Roller	162, 163, 165–167
" Sensible	168
" " Combination Loop	169
" Shoe or Skate	163
" Trace, Horse Shoe	170
" " Barrel Roller	170
" Philadelphia	171
Buttons, Door	116
" Trunk	252
Butts, Acorn, Drilled	5
" Bronze-Metal	2
" Bronzed	3
" Narrow, Cast	6, 7
" " " Drilled	12, 13
" Broad, "	8, 9
" " " Drilled	14, 15
" Loose Pin, Drilled	4
" Lull & Porter's	20, 21
" Mayer's	10
" " Drilled	16
" Parliament	11
" " Drilled	17
" Wrought	18, 19

C

Carriage Bands	193–199
" Castings	200–231
" Dove-Tails	183
" Hinges	182

	PAGE
Carriage Wrenches	200
Casters, Bed	128
" Box	130
" Bracket	129
" French	127
" Piano	126
" Plate	126
" Sewing Machine	129
" Socket	127
Catches, Window and Cupboard	104, 105
Ceiling Hooks	88, 89
Chain Bolts	65
" Door Fasteners	58, 59
" Swivels	238, 239
Chest Handles	97, 99
" Rollers	113
Clamps, Cloth	119
" Screw	188
" Quilting Frame	119
Cleats	122
Clevices, Plough	232
Clinch Rings	241
Clothes-Line Hooks	90–93
" " Pulleys	56
Couch Hinges	182
Coal-Hod Ears and Handles	256
Coal Shovels	258
Coat and Hat Hooks	78–83
Cock Eyes, Screw	178
" Triangular	178
Coffee-Pot Stands	145
Cork Pressers	144
Crabs, Pole	235
Cupboard Catches	104, 105
" Knobs	108
Cutters, Tobacco	133

D

D's, Harness	181
Damper Handles	253
Dampers, Stove-Pipe	258
Dish-Pan Handles	257
Door Knockers	115

	PAGE
Door Buttons	116
" Pulls	118
" Sheaves, Sliding	57
Dove-Tails, Carriage	183
" Trunk	244, 245
Drawer Pulls	100–103, 118
Drop Thumb Latches	67
Druggists' Brackets	154
Dumb Bells	149
" Waiter Pulleys	55

E

Ears, Bucket, Coal-Hod & Kettle	254–256
Ends, Roller	136, 137
Eyes, Hatch Rope	125

F

Fasteners, Bedstead	131, 132
" Chain, Door	58, 59
" Hame	179
" Sash	106, 107, 110
" Shutter, Inside	75
" " and Outside	75
Felloe Plates, Wrought-Iron	223
Fence Staples	114
Fire Detectors	132
Floor Nails	261
Foot Rests	146
Foot Scrapers	140, 141
Frame Pulleys	31, 39
French Casters	127
Friction Rollers	143

G

Garden Hoes	143
" Rakes	143
Gate Hinges	21
" Knockers	115
" Latches	22
Grindstone Fixtures	142
Gridirons	144
Groovers, Roofing	258
Gum Spring Hooks	83

H

	PAGE
Halter Bolts	180
" Squares	180
" Triangles	181
Hame Castings	236, 237
Hame Fasteners	179
Handles, Chest	97, 99
" Coal-Hod	256
" Damper	263
" Dish-Pan	257
" Milk Can	259
" Sauce-Pan	253
" Water Cooler, etc.	260, 261
Hangers, Barn Door	34–39
Harness Buckles	164, 168
" Rings	162
" D's	161
" Hooks	86, 87
Hasps, Hinge	114
Hat and Coat Hooks	78, 83
Hatch Rope Eyes	125
Hay-Fork Pulleys	151
Head-Board Hooks and Eyes	85
Hinges, Carriage and Coach	182
" Bronze-Metal, Butt	2
" Bronzed	3
" Butt, Acorn, Drilled	5
" " Loose-Pin, Drilled	4
" " Narrow	6, 7
" " " Drilled	12, 13
" " Broad	3, 9
" " " Drilled	14, 15
" Gate	21
" Lall & Porter's	20, 21
" Mayer's	10
" " Drilled	16
" Parliament	11
" " Drilled	17
" Trunk	250
" Wrought	18, 19
Hoes, Garden	143
" Potato	143
Hooks, Awning	96

	PAGE
Hooks Bird-Cage	93, 94
" Ceiling	88, 89
" Clothes-Line	90–93
" Gum-Spring	85
" Harness	86, 87
" Hat and Coat	78–83
" Hat-Rack	95
" Lamp	96
" Picture	96
" School-House	84
" Shutter, Malleable	75
" Wardrobe	76, 77
" and-Eyes, Head-Board	85
Hydrant Handles	264
" Stays	264

J

Jump Seat Irons	185

K

Kettle Ears	254, 255
Knobs, Cupboard	105
" Lid	253
" Shutter, Bronzed	108
" Stove	260
Knockers, Door and Gate	115

L

Ladles, Melting	150
Lamp Hooks	96
Latches, Barn-Door	71
" Gate	22
" Store-Door	68, 69
" " Bronzed	70
" Thumb	66
" " Cast	66
" " Drop	67
Lathe Carriers	149
Lazy Back Irons	184
Lemon Squeezers	146, 147
Letter-Box Plates	131
Lifts, Sash	111
" Shutter	112

	PAGE
Loop Buckles, Combination, Sensible	169
Loops, Breeching	179
" Trace	180
Lull & Porter's Hinges	20, 21

M

Mall'ble Iron Car'age Castings, etc.	200-231
Malleable Castings for Tin and Sheet-Iron Workers, Plumbers, etc	253-264
Mantel Brackets	161
Mayer's Hinges	10
" " Drilled	16
Melting Ladles	150
Meter Wrenches	264
Milk-Can Handles and Holders	259
Mortice Gate Latches	22

N

Neck Bolts, Wrought	62
Nuts, Thumb	240

O

Oar Locks	120
Ox Balls	152

P

Parliament Hinges	11
" " Drilled	17
Piano Casters	126
Picture Hooks	96
Plate Casters	126
Plough Clevises	232
Plumb Bobs	117
Pole Crabs	235
" Tips	187, 235
" Brackets	180
Porch Post-Supporters	23
Potato Hoes	143
Pressers, Cork	144
Props, Sash	110
" Top	189, 191
Pulleys, Axle	40-50

	PAGE
Pulleys, Bell	31
" Clothes Line	56
" Dumb Waiter	55
" Frame	31, 39
" Hay-Fork	151
" Screw	51-53
" Side	54
" Upright	55
Pulls, Door	118
" Drawer	100-103, 118

Q

Quilting-Frame Clamps	119
Quoits	149

R

Racks, Window-Shade	138
Rails, Barn-Door	30
" Sheave	57
Rakes, Garden	143
Rein Swivels	176
Rings, Galvanized	125
" Japanned and Tinned	162
Rods, Saw	115
Roller Ends	136, 137
Roller Buckles	162, 163, 165-167
Rollers, Barn-Door	30
" Chest	113
" Friction	143
" Sash	113
" Trunk	248, 249
Roofing Groovers	258
Row Locks	120
Rosettes for Shutter Stays	72
Rudder Braces	121

S

Sad-Iron Stands	145
Sash Fasteners	106, 107, 110
" Lifts	111
" Props	110
" Rollers	113
Satchel Plates	252

INDEX.

	PAGE
Sauce-Pan Handles	253
Saw Rods	115
School-House Hooks	84
Scrapers, Foot	140, 141
Screw Clamps	188
" Cock Eyes	178
" Pulleys	51, 53
Shackles, Spring	243
Shade Brackets	134, 135
" -Cord Holders	137
" Racks	138
" Roller Ends	136, 137
Shaft Tips	187, 235
Shaw's Patent Ferrules	232
Sheave Rail	57
" Wheels	117
Sheaves, Sliding-Door	57
Shelf Brackets	155–159
Shifting Top Plates	241
Shoe Buckles	163
Shovels, Coal	258
Shutter Bars	109
" Bolts, Cast	60
" " Wrought	62
" Bowers	71
" Fasteners	75
" Hooks	75
" Knobs	108
" Lifts	112
" Screws	113
" Stays	72, 74
" -Stay Rosettes	72
Side Pulleys	54
Skate Buckles	163
Soap Cups	139
Socket Casters	127
Spittoons	139
Spring Bolts	61
" Shackles	243
Squares, Halter	180
Squeezers, Cork	144
" Lemon	146, 147
Stands, Coffee-Pot	145

	PAGE
Stands, Sad-Iron	145
" Umbrella	153
Staples for Spring Bolts	64
" for Wire Fence	114
Stay Nails	117
Stays, Shutter	72–74
Stirrups	181
Store-Door Latches	68, 69
" " Bronzed	70
Stove Knobs	260
Stove-Pipe Dampers	258
Stove Turnbuckles	262
Stubs and Plates	112
Supporters, Porch-Post	23
" Table-Leaf	118
Swingletree Tips	186, 234
Swivels, Chain	238, 239
" Rein	176

T

Table-Leaf Supports	118
Table Hinges, Wrought-Iron	19
Tackle Blocks	123
Terrets	177
Thimbles, Malleable-Iron	124
Thumb Latches	66
" Nuts	240
" Screws	241
Tips, Pole	187, 235
" Shaft	187, 235
" Swingletree	186, 234
" Yoke	186, 234
Tobacco Cutters	133
Top Props	189–191
Top-Prop Nuts and Rivets	191
Tower Bolts	60
Transom Plates	112
Triangular Cock-Eyes	178
Truck Wheels	130
Trunk Bottoms	252
" Handle Caps	251
" " Loops	252
" Hinges	250

	PAGE		PAGE
Trunk Dove-Tails	244, 245	Wash-Pave Keys	264
" Plates	246	Washers, Cast-Iron	242
" Rollers	248, 249	" Thornley's	242
Turn Buckles	72-74	" Clinch	241

U

		Water-Cooler Handles	260, 261
		Wheels, Sheave	117
Umbrella Stands	153	" Truck	130
Upright Pulleys	55	" Well	150

V

		Window Catches	104
		Wrenches	200, 201
Ventilators	116	" Meter	264

W

Y

Wall Nails	261		
Wardrobe Hooks	76, 77	Yoke Tips	186, 234

TERMS CASH

Bills remaining unpaid after the lapse of the customary thirty days' average, will be drawn for at sight, with three days' notice.

Prices subject to change without notice.

No charge will be made for packages when goods are ordered in full cases or barrels, as set forth through the Catalogue. A reasonable charge will be made, however, for packages containing assorted goods.

BRONZE METAL LOOSE PIN BUTTS.

WITH BRASS SCREWS AND STEEL WASHERS.

No. 105.

[BLANK PAGE]

CARR, CRAWLEY & DEVLIN'S CATALOGUE.

BRONZE METAL LOOSE PIN BUTTS.
WITH BRASS SCREWS AND STEEL WASHERS.

No. 106.

3 by 3 inches		$3.60	per pair.
3½ " 3½ "		4.00	"
4 4		5.20	"
4½ 4½		6.00	"
5 5		6.80	"
5½ 5½		8.40	"
6 " 6 "		10.00	"

3

BRONZED LOOSE PIN BUTTS.

WITH BRONZED SCREWS.

Nos. 95 and 100.

No. 95, Bronzed		No. 100, Polished and Bronzed.
3 by 3 inches	$1.30 per pair	$1.50 per pair.
3½ " 3½ "	1.45 "	1.70 "
4 " 4 "	1.60 "	1.90 "
4½ " 4½ "	1.80 "	2.10 "
5 " 5 "	2.15 "	2.50 "
5½ " 5½ "	2.55 "	3.00 "
6 " 6 "	3.00 "	3.50 "

LOOSE PIN PANEL BUTTS.

DRILLED.

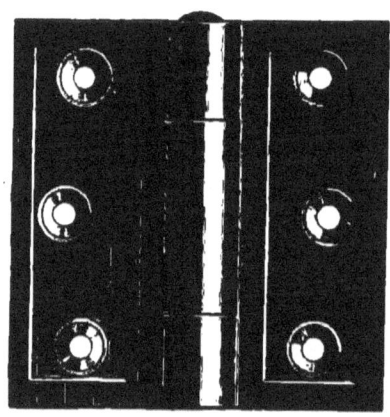

No. 15.

2 by 2 inches	$1.00 per dozen.	3½ by 4 inches	$2.50 per dozen.
2½ " 2	1.20 "	4 " 3½	2.70 "
2½ " 2½	1.35 "	4 " 4	2.90 "
3 " 2½	1.60 "	4 " 4½	3.20 "
3 " 3	1.75 "	4½ " 4	3.50 "
3 " 3½	1.95 "	4½ " 4½	4.00 "
3½ " 3	2.15 "	5 " 5	5.50 "
3½ " 3½	2.35 "		

ACORN BUTTS.

LOOSE PIN. DRILLED.

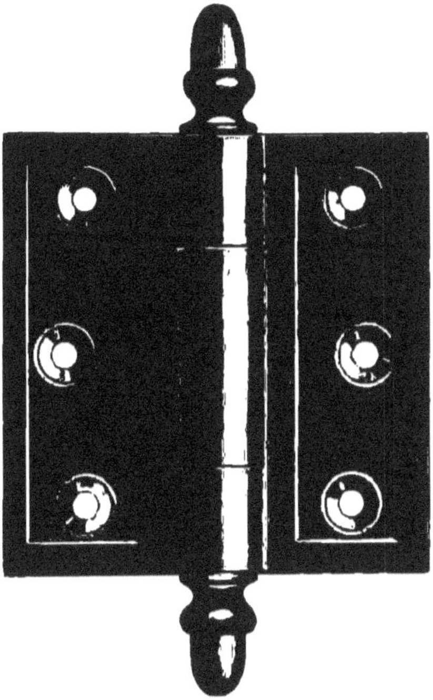

	No. 20. Not Jap'nd.	No. 25. Jap'nd.	No. 30. Japanned with Silvered tips.
2 by 2 inches,	$1.00	$2.50	$5.60 pr doz.
2 " 2½ "	1.10	2.65	5.80 "
2½ " 2 "	1.20	2.80	6.00 "
2½ " 2½ "	1.35	3.00	6.20 "
2½ " 3 "	1.50	3.15	6.30 "
3 " 2½ "	1.60	3.30	6.40 "
3 " 3 "	1.75	3.50	6.50 "
3 " 3½ "	1.95	3.65	7.00 "
3½ " 3 "	2.15	3.80	7.50 "
3½ " 3½ "	2.35	4.00	8.00 "
3½ " 4 "	2.50	4.40	8.40 "
4 " 3½ "	2.70	4.70	8.80 "

	No. 20. Not Jap'nd.	No. 25. Jap'nd.	No. 30. Japanned with Silvered tips.
4 by 4 inches,	$2.90	$5.00	$9.20 pr doz.
4 " 4½ "	3.20	5.40	9.50 "
4½ " 4 "	3.50	5.70	9.70 "
4½ " 4½ "	4.00	6.00	10.00 "
4½ " 5 "	4.20	6.60	10.80 "
5 " 4½ "	5.00	7.00	11.60 "
5 " 5 "	5.50	7.50	12.50 "
5 " 5½ "	5.70	8.00	13.00 "
5½ " 5 "	6.00	8.50	13.50 "
5½ " 5½ "	6.50	9.00	14.00 "
6 " 6 "	7.60	11.00	16.00 "

48 dozen in a case of 2 by 2, to 2½ by 2½.
24 " " " " 2½ by 3, to 4 by 3½.
12 " " " " 4 by 4, to 6 by 6.

CAST BUTTS.

FAST.

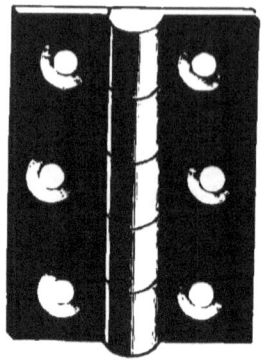

No. 35.

1 inch	80 45	per dozen.
1¼ inches	48	"
1½ "	50	"
1¾ "	55	"
2 "	60	"
2¼ "	65	"
2½ "	70	"
2¾ "	80	"
3 "	95	"

48 DOZEN IN A CASE.

3½ inches	$1 20	per dozen.
4 "	1 40	"
4½ "	1 90	"
5 "	2 30	"

24 DOZEN IN A CASE.

CAST BUTTS

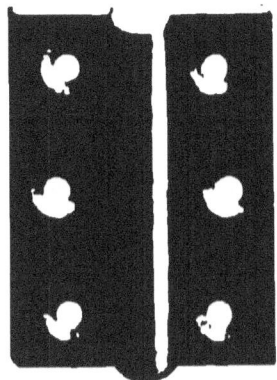

CAST BUTTS.

FAST.

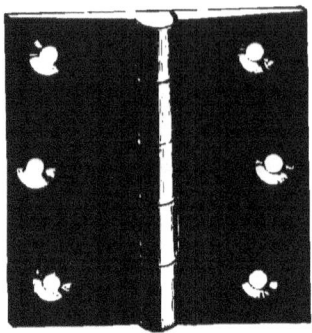

No. 45.

2 by 2 inches		$1 00	per dozen
2 " 2¼ "		1 10	"
2¼ " 2¼ "		1 20	"
2¼ " 2½ "		1 35	"

48 DOZEN IN A CASE.

2½ by 3 inches		$1 50	per dozen
3 " 2½ "		1 60	"
3 " 3 "		1 75	"
3 " 3½ "		1 95	"
3½ " 3 "		2 15	"
3½ " 3½ "		2 35	"

24 DOZEN IN A CASE.

3½ by 4 inches		$2 50	per dozen
4 " 3½ "		2 70	"
4 " 4 "		2 90	"
4 " 4½ "		3 20	"
4½ " 4 "		3 50	"
4½ " 4½ "		4 00	"
5 " 5 "		5 40	"
5½ " 5½ "		6 50	"
6 " 6 "		7 60	"

12 DOZEN IN A CASE.

CAST BUTTS.

LOOSE.

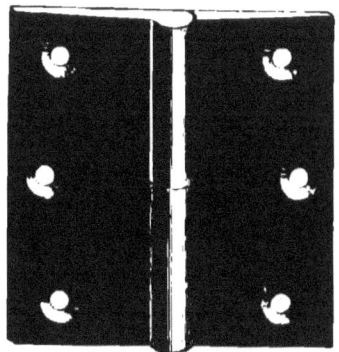

No. 50.

2 by 2 inches			$1 00	per dozen.
2 " 2¼	"		1 10	"
2½ " 2	"		1 20	"
2½ " 2¼	"		1 35	"

48 DOZEN IN A CASE

2½ by 3 inches			$1 50	per dozen.
3 " 2½	"		1 60	"
3 " 3	"		1 75	"
3 " 3½	"		1 95	"
3½ " 3	"		2 15	
3½ " 3½	"		2 35	

24 DOZEN IN A CASE

3½ by 4 inches			$2 50	per dozen.
4 " 3½	"		2 70	"
4 " 4	"		2 90	"
4 " 4½	"		3 20	"
4½ " 4	"		3 50	"
4½ " 4½	"		4 00	"
5 " 5	"		5 50	"
5½ " 5½	"		6 50	
6 " 6	"		7 60	

12 DOZEN IN A CASE.

MAYER'S HINGES.

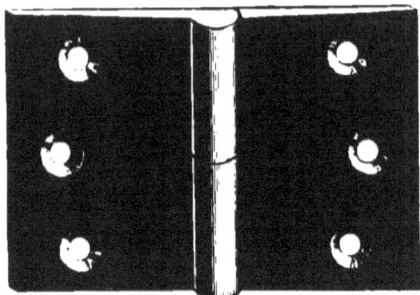

No. 55.

No. 0, 2 by 3 inches	$1 50	per dozen.
" 1, 2¼ " 3½ "	1 60	"
" 2, 2½ " 3	1 90	"
" 3, 2¾ " 4	2 20	"

24 DOZEN IN A CASE.

No. 4, 3 by 4 inches	$2 75	per dozen.
5, 3¼ " 4½ "	3 20	"
6, 3½ " 4½ "	4 00	"
" 12, 2½ " 4½ "	2 67	"

12 DOZEN IN A CASE.

GALVANIZED.

No. 0	$3 33	per dozen.
" 1	4 17	"
2	4 75	"
3	6 00	"
4	6 67	"
5	7 00	"
" 6	7 50	"
" 12	6 50	"

PARLIAMENT HINGES.

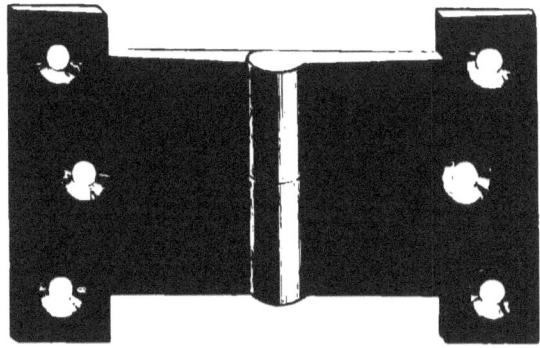

No. 60.

3 inches	$1 20	per dozen.
3½ "	1 45	"
4 "	1 90	"
4½ "	2 00	"
5 "	2 20	"
5½ "	2 40	"
6 "	2 80	"

24 DOZEN IN A CASE.

6½ inches	$3 20	per dozen.
7 "	3 80	"
8 "	4 40	"

12 DOZEN IN A CASE.

CAST BUTTS.

FAST.

DRILLED AND WIRE JOINTED.

No. 65.

$0 48 per dozen.
50 "
55 "
60
65
70
80
95

48 DOZEN IN A CASE.

$1 20 per dozen
1 40 "
1 90
2 30

CAST BUTTS.

LOOSE.

DRILLED AND WIRE JOINTED.

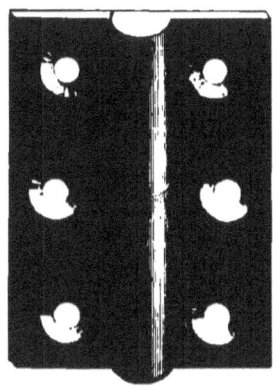

No. 70.

2 inches		$1 00	per dozen.
2½ "		1 10	"
3 "		1 50	"

48 DOZEN IN A CASE.

3½ inches		$1 75	per dozen.
4 "		2 10	"

24 DOZEN IN A CASE.

CAST BUTTS.

FAST.

DRILLED AND WIRE JOINTED.

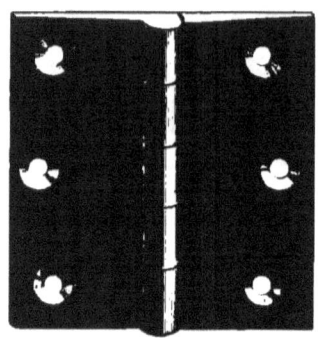

No. 75.

2 by 2 inches	$1 00	per dozen
2 " 2¼ "	1 10	"
2¼ " 2 "	1 20	"
2¼ " 2¼ "	1 35	"

48 DOZEN IN A CASE.

2½ by 3 inches	$1 50	per dozen
3 " 2½ "	1 60	"
3 " 3 "	1 75	"
3 " 3½ "	1 95	"
3½ " 3 "	2 15	"
3½ " 3½ "	2 35	"

24 DOZEN IN A CASE.

3 by 4 inches	$2 50	per dozen
4 " 3½ "	2 70	"
4 " 4 "	2 90	"
4 " 4½ "	3 20	"
4 " 4 "	3 50	"
4½ " 4½ "	4 00	"
5 " 5 "	5 50	"
5½ " 5½ "	6 50	"
6 " 6 "	7 60	"

12 DOZEN IN A CASE.

CAST BUTTS.

LOOSE.

DRILLED AND WIRE JOINTED.

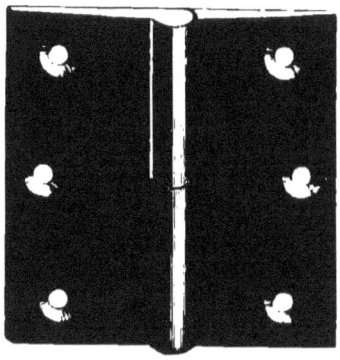

No. 80.

2 by 2	Inches	$1 00	per dozen.
2 " 2¼	"	1 10	"
2¼ " 2	"	1 20	"
2¼ " 2¼	"	1 35	"

48 DOZEN IN A CASE.

2½ by 3	Inches	$1 50	per dozen.
3 " 2½	"	1 60	"
3 " 3	"	1 75	"
3 " 3½	"	1 95	
3½ " 3	"	2 15	
3½ " 3½	"	2 35	

24 DOZEN IN A CASE.

3½ by 4	Inches	$2 50	per dozen.
4 " 3½	"	2 70	"
4 " 4	"	2 90	"
4 " 4½	"	3 20	"
4½ " 4	"	3 50	"
4½ " 4½	"	4 00	"
5 " 5	"	5 50	"
5½ " 5½	"	6 50	"
6 " 6	"	7 00	"

12 DOZEN IN A CASE.

MAYER'S HINGES.

DRILLED AND WIRE JOINTED.

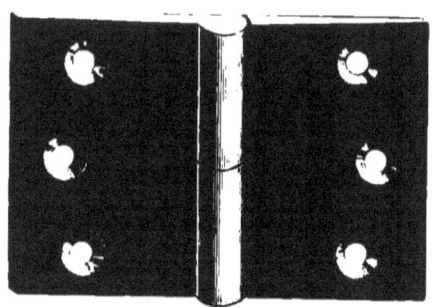

No. 85.

No. 0, 2 by 3½ inches	$1 50	per dozen.
" 1, 2½ " 3½ "	1 60	"
" 2, 2½ " 3½ "	1 90	"
" 3, 2½ " 4 "	2 20	"

24 DOZEN IN A CASE.

No. 4, 3 by 4½ inches	$2 75	per dozen.
" 5, 3½ " 4½ "	3 20	"
" 6, 3½ " 4½ "	4 00	"
" 12, 2½ " 4½ "	2 67	"

12 DOZEN IN A CASE.

GALVANIZED.

No. 0	$3 33	per dozen.
1	4 17	"
2	4 75	"
3	6 00	"
4	6 67	"
5	7 00	"
6	7 50	"
" 12	6 50	"

PARLIAMENT HINGES.

DRILLED AND WIRE JOINTED

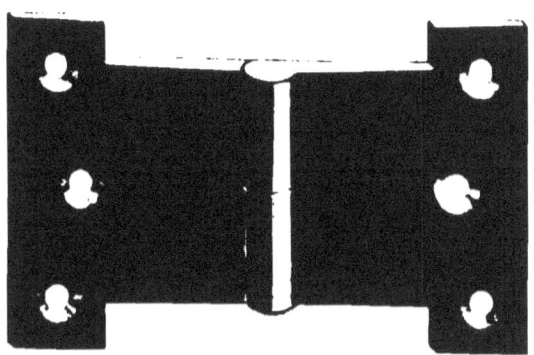

No. 90.

4 inches
4½ "
5 "
5½ "
6 "
6½ "
7 "

24 DOZEN IN A CASE.

6½ inches
7 "
8 "

12 DOZEN IN A CASE.

Wrought Iron Inside Blind Hinges.

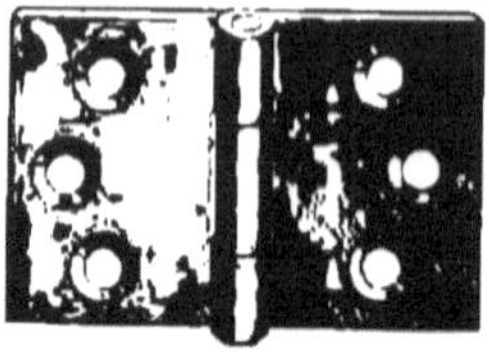

No. 110.

	1	1 1/8	1 1/4	1 3/8	1 1/2	1 3/4	inches.
Polished	$0 45	$0 50	$0 55	$0 60	$0 65	$0 75	per dozen.
Bronzed, with Screws	1 70	1 80	1 90	2 05	2 20	2 50	"

Wrought Iron Butts.

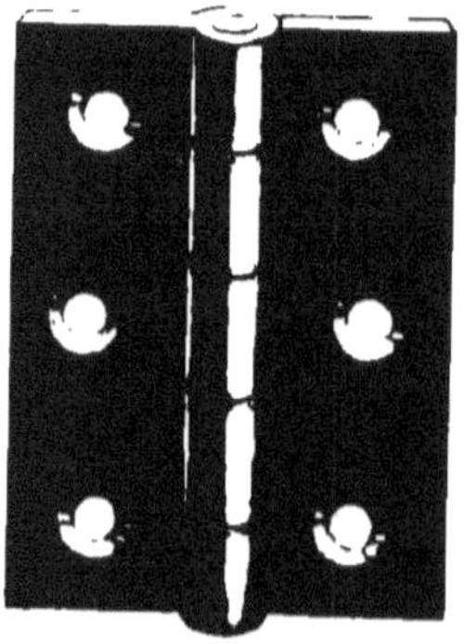

No 115.

	1	1 1/4	1 1/2	1 3/4	2	2 1/4	2 1/2	2 3/4	3	3 1/4	3 1/2	4	inches.
Plain	$0 32	$0 36	$0 43	$0 50	$0 60	$0 66	$0 72	$0 84	$0 90	$1 08	$1 44	$1 90	per dozen.
Bronzed, with Screws	1 30	1 40	1 50	1 65	1 85	2 05	2 25						

Wrought Iron Back Flaps.

SQUARE.

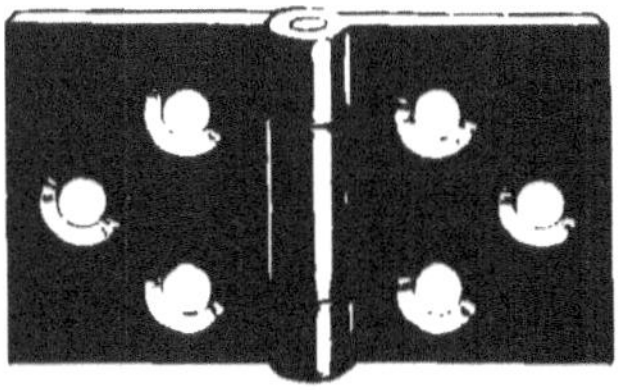

No. 120.

$0 45	$0 50	$0 55	$0 60	$0 65	$0 75 per dozen.
1	1⅛	1¼	1⅜	1½	1¾ inch.

Wrought Iron Table Hinges.

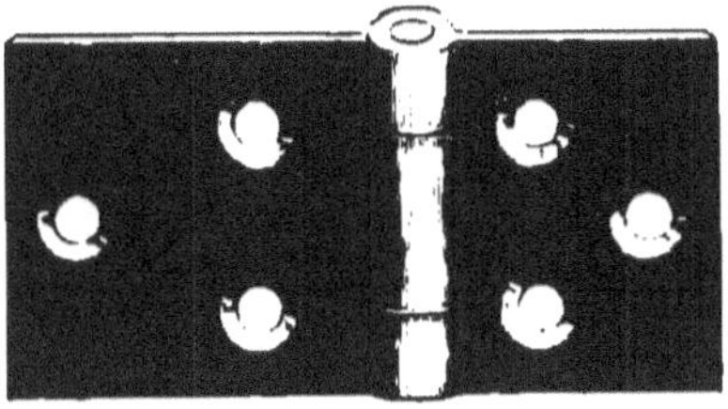

No. 125.

$0 43	$0 45	$0 50	$0 55	$0 60	$0 65	$0 80 per dozen.
⅞	1	1⅛	1¼	1⅜	1½	1¾ inch.

Wrought Iron Back Flaps.

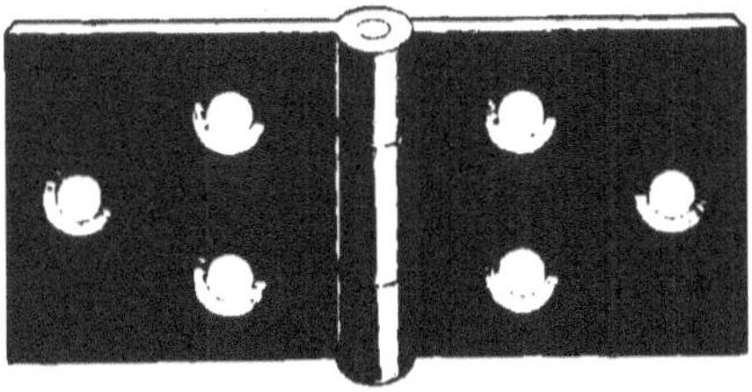

No. 130.

$0 47	$0 50	$0 55	$0 60	$0 65	$0 70	$0 80 per dozen.
⅞	1	1⅛	1¼	1⅜	1½	1¾ inch.

LULL & PORTER'S

PATENT

Self-Fastening Shutter Hinges.

No. 640 with inside fastenings, 10 inches, when open,............ $12 00 per dozen pairs—35 lbs.
" 540   "   "   9 "   "   .... 11 00   "   "   32 "
" 440   "   "   8½ "   "   .... 10 00   "   "   30 "
" 340   "   "   7½ "   "   9 00   "   "   27½ "
" 240   "   "   7 "   "   .... 8 00   "   "   26½ "
"   0,   "   "   6¼ "   "   5 25   "   "   26 "
"   1,   "   "   5½ "   "   4 50   "   "   25 "
"   1½, "   "   5 "   "   4 25   "   "   20½ "
"   2,   "   "   4½ "   "   3 90   "   "   18 "
"   2½, "   "   3½ "   "   3 50   "   "   12½ "
"   3   "   "   3¼ "   "   3 15   "   "   11 "

12 DOZEN PAIRS IN A CASE.

LULL & PORTER'S
PATENT
Self-Fastening Shutter Hinges.
SURFACE.

No. 3¼, equivalent to 3 inches, with inside fastenings,.................... .... $3 00 per dozen pairs.
" 4½,   "   4   "   "   "   .... 3 50   "
" 5¼,   "   5   "   "   "   .... 4 00   "

12 DOZEN PAIRS IN A CASE.

GATE HINGES.
SELF-CLOSING, FOR RIGHT OR LEFT HAND.

No. 3 Latch.

No. 1, with Latches.. $7 50 per dozen sets.
" 11, without   " .... 6 10   "
" 2, with   " .... 8 25   "
" 12, without   " .... 6 85   "

GATE LATCHES.

No. 4.

No. 4, Japanned, surface... $1 60 per dozen.
 "   5, mortice.. 1 40   "
 "   1, rivetted, mortice... 1 80   "
 " 11, rivetted and japanned, mortice................................ 2 00   "
 "   2,   "   "   7 inch Lever, mortice....................... 3 00   "

PORCH-POST SUPPORTERS.

JAPANNED.

No. 1.   *No. 2.*   *No. 3.*

Nos. 4 and 5.   *No. 7.*

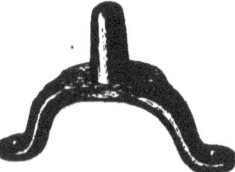 

No. 1,	$2 25 per dozen.
" 2,	2 80 "
" 3,	4 00 "
" 4,	1 80 "
" 5,	2 10 "
" 7,	2 80 "

BARN DOOR HANGERS.

No. 4.

3 inch Wheel, 10 inch Strap,		$0 35 per pair.
4	"	11	"	45 "
5	"	12	"	60 "
6	"	14	"	75 "
8	"	16	"	1 00 "

BARN DOOR HANGERS.

No. 2.

3 inch Wheel, 10 inch Strap			$0 56	per pair.
4 "	11 "		70	"
5 "	13 "		90	"
6 "	15½ "		1 20	"
7 "	19 "		2 25	"

BARN DOOR HANGERS.

No 1.

FOR FLAT OR ANGLE RAIL.

3 inch Wheel, 13 inch Strap	$0 65	per pair.
4 " 16 "	95	"
5 " 18 "	1 30	"
6 " 19½ "	1 62	"

BARN DOOR HANGERS.

No. 5.

FOR FLAT OR ANGLE RAIL.

3 inch Wheel, 10 inch Strap,	....	6 lbs.	$0 65	per pair.
4 "	13 "	....	8 "	95	"
5 "	15 "	....	12½ "	1 30	"
6 "	18 "	....	18 "	1 62	"

BARN DOOR HANGERS.

No. 3.

3 inch Wheel, 13 inch Strap	....	$0 90	per pair.
4 " 16 "	....	1 20	"
5 " 18 "	....	1 75	"
6 " 19½ "	....	2 25	"
6 " 28 "	....	2 85	"

BARN DOOR HANGERS.

No. 6.

3 inch Wheel, Groove ⅞ inch deep, 13 inch Strap,..................................... $0 95 per pair.
4   "   "   "   "   "   16   "   .... 1 30   "
5   "   "   "   "   "   18   "   .... 1 85   "
6   "   "   "   "   "   19½ "   .... 2 35   "
8   "   "   "   "   "   28   "   .... 4 00   "

BARN DOOR ROLLERS.

| $0 35 | $0 45 | $0 60 | $1 00 | $1 50 per pair. |
| 4 | 5 | 6 | 8 | 10 inch. |

BARN DOOR RAIL.

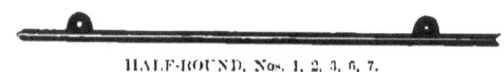

HALF-ROUND, Nos. 1, 2, 3, 6, 7.

FLAT, No. 4.

BELL PULLEYS.

1¼ inch, ... $0 25 per dozen.

FRAME PULLEYS.

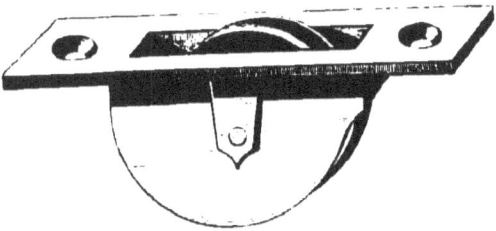

No. 0, 1¼ inch .... $0 28 per dozen.

100 DOZEN IN A CASE.

FRAME PULLEYS.

                        Papered—in Cases of 100 doz.   Loose in barrels of 175 doz.
No. 3, 1¼ inch ....$0 32 $0 30 per dozen.

Nos. 15, 20 and 25.

                       Papered—in Cases of 100 doz.   Loose—in Barrels of 180 doz.
No. 15, 1¼ inch .... $0 43 $0 41 per dozen.
" 20, " Polished Wheel 46   44 "
" 25, " " painted face 50   48 "

FRAME PULLEYS.

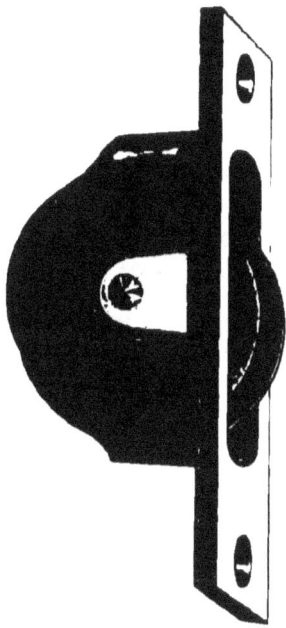

Nos. 106, 107 and 108.

	Papered—In Cases of 100 doz.	Loose—In Barrels of 130 dozen.
No. 106, 1¾ inch	$0 45	$0 43 per dozen.
" 107, " Painted Face	48	46 "
" 108, " " Polished Wheel	52	50 "

FRAME PULLEYS.

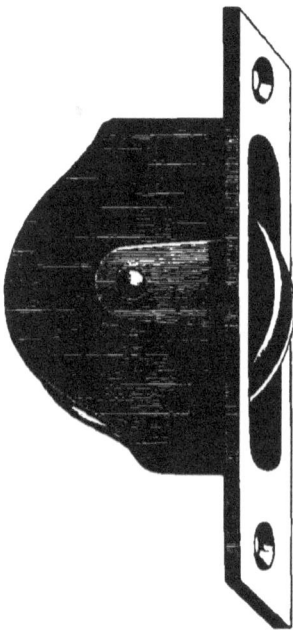

Nos. 109, 110 and 112.

	Papered—In Cases of 50 doz.	Loose—In Barrels of 100 doz.
No. 109, 2 inch	$0 54	$0 52 per dozen.
" 110, " Painted Face	57	55 "
" 112, " " Polished Wheel	61	59 "

FRAME PULLEYS.

No. 2, 1¾ inch, Painted Face,..$0 63 per dozen.

50 DOZEN IN A CASE.

FRAME PULLEYS.

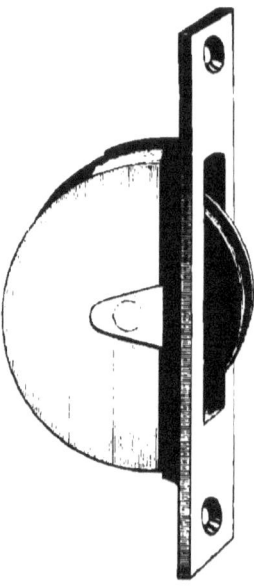

Nos. 1, 11 and 12.

No. 1, 1¼ inch, Painted Face		$0 48 per dozen.
" 11, " Turned and Polished Wheel, Painted Face		90	"
" 12, " " " " Bronzed "		1 10	"

50 DOZEN IN A CASE.

FRAME PULLEYS.

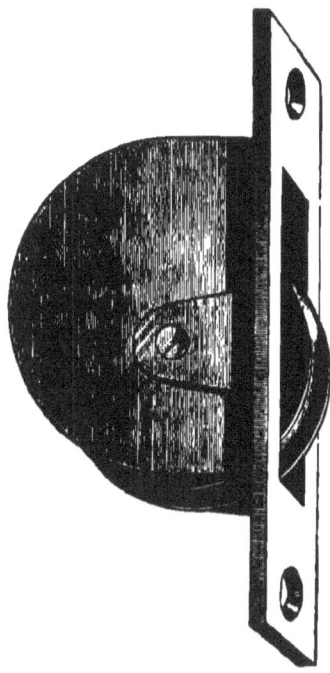

Nos. 21, 31, 41 and 51.

No. 21, 2 inch, Painted Face, Iron Pin... $0 75 per dozen.
" 31, "   Turned and Polished Wheel, Painted Face, Iron Pin.......... 1 25 "
" 41, "   "   "   "   Bronzed "   "   .... 1 50 "
" 51, "   "   "   "   "   "   " Brass Pin......... 2 00 "

50 DOZEN IN A CASE.

FRAME PULLEYS.

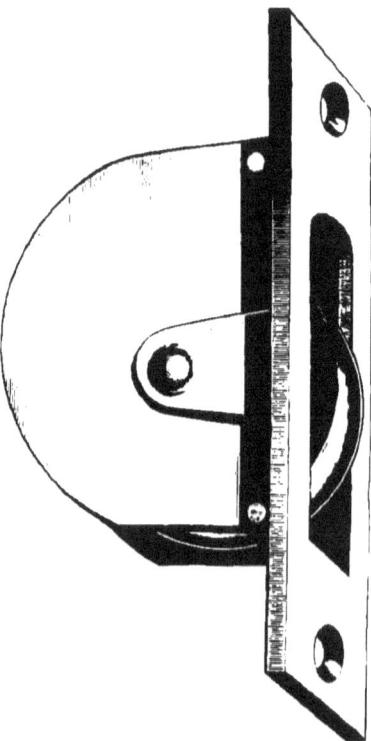

Nos. 61, 71 and 81.

No. 61, 2¼ inch Turned and Polished Wheel, Painted Face, ¼ inch Iron Pin, $2 00 per dozen.
" 71, " " " " Bronzed " " " 2 50 "
" 81, " " " " " " " Brass Pin, 3 50 "

FRAME PULLEYS.

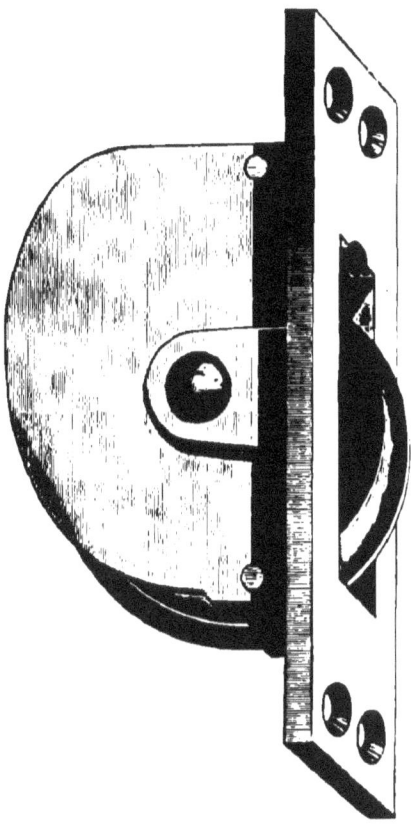

Nos. 91, 101 and 111.

No. 91, 2¼ inch, Turned and Polished Wheel, Painted Face, ⅝ inch Iron Pin,...... $3 50 per dozen.
" 101,   "   "   "   "   Bronzed   "   "   "   ...... 4 25   "
" 111,   "   "   "   "   "   "   "   Brass Pin,..... 6 00   "

AXLE PULLEYS.

No. 115, 1¾ inch Painted Face .... $0 53 per dozen.

100 DOZEN IN A CASE.

AXLE PULLEYS.

No 118, 1¾ inch, Painted Face...$0 62 per dozen.

100 DOZEN IN A CASE.

AXLE PULLEYS.

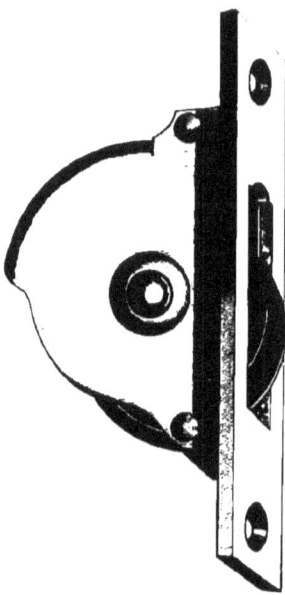

Nos. 5 and 105.

No. 5, 1¼ inch, Milled Axle, Painted Face................................. $0 64 per dozen.
" 105, "   "   "   Polished Wheel.................... 70   "

100 DOZEN IN A CASE.

AXLE PULLEYS.

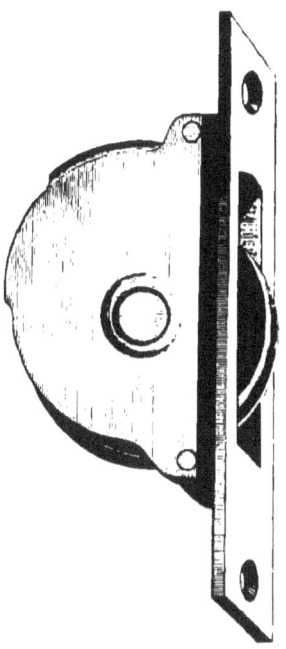

No. 13, 2 inch, Painted Face .... 80 60 per dozen.

50 DOZEN IN A CASE.

AXLE PULLEYS.

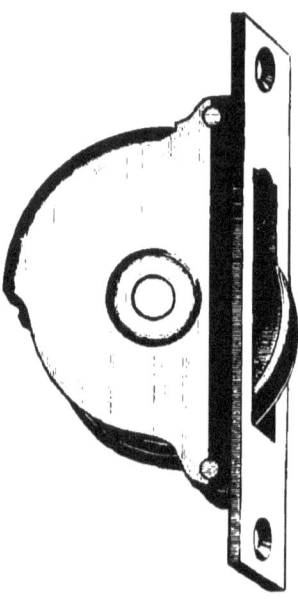

Nos. 4 and 104.

No. 4, 2 inch, Milled Axle, Painted Face .... $0 68 per dozen.
" 104, "   "   "   Polished Wheel .... 75 "

50 DOZEN IN A CASE.

AXLE PULLEYS.

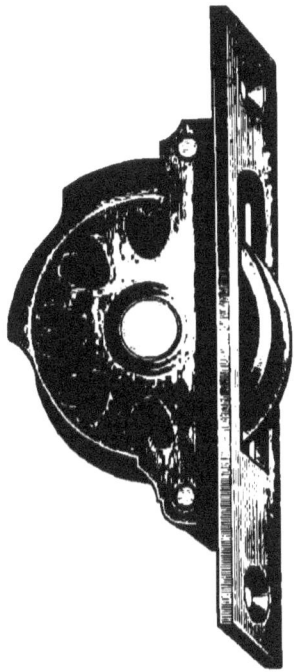

Nos. 119 and 119½.

No. 119, 2 inch, Milled Axle, Painted Face............................... $0 70 per dozen.
" 119½, "   "   "   Polished Wheel.................   77   "

50 DOZEN IN A CASE.

AXLE PULLEYS.

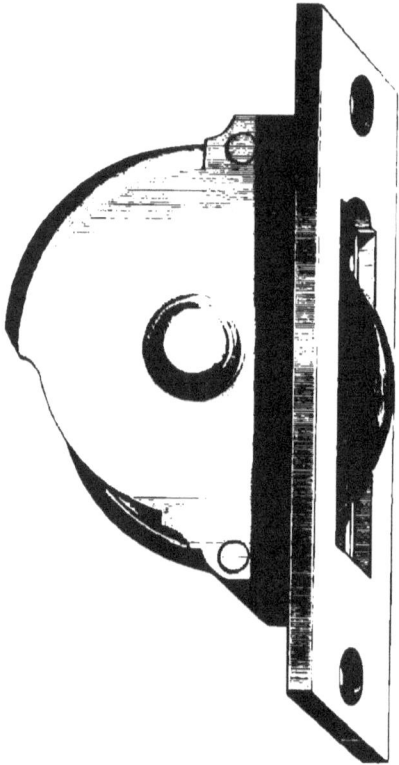

Nos. 6 and 16.

No. 6, 2¼ inch, Milled Axle, Painted Face .... $1 35 per dozen.
" 16, " " " .... 1 50 "

50 DOZEN IN A CASE.

AXLE PULLEYS.

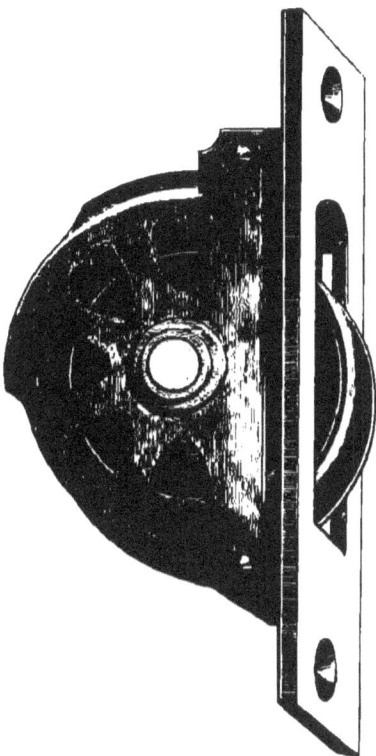

Nos. 120 and 121.

No. 120, 2¼ inch, Milled Axle, Painted Face.. $1 00 per dozen.
" 121, "   "   "   .... 1 15   "

50 DOZEN IN A CASE.

AXLE PULLEYS.

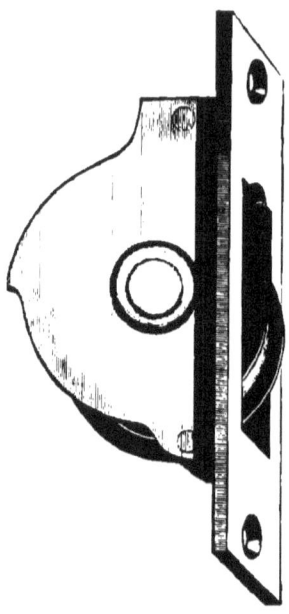

Nos. 72 and 73.

No. 72, 1¾ inch, Turned & Polished Wheel, Milled Axle, Painted Face ....$1 25 per doz.
" 73,   "   "   "   "   "   "   Polished & Bronzed Face 1 46   "

50 DOZEN IN A CASE.

AXLE PULLEYS.

Nos. 74 and 75.

No. 74, 2 inch, Turned & Polished Wheel, Milled Axle, Painted Face ...... $1 45 per doz.
" 75, "   "   "   "   "   Polished & Bronzed Face 2 65 "

50 DOZEN IN A CASE.

AXLE PULLEYS.

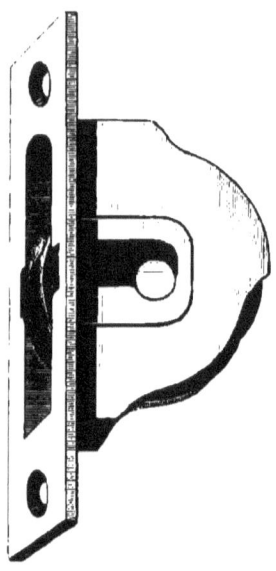

No. 50, 2 inch .... $0 60 per dozen.

50 DOZEN IN A CASE.

SCREW PULLEYS.

1½ inch
1¼ "
1 "
2½ "
2¼ "
2 "
3 "
4 "

SHIELD SCREW PULLEYS.

2 inches, Japanned .... $1 50 per dozen.
2½   "   "   .... 2 00   "

ENCASED SCREW PULLEYS.

2½ inches, Japanned .... $3 00 per dozen.
5   "   "   .... 13 00   "

SIDE PULLEYS.

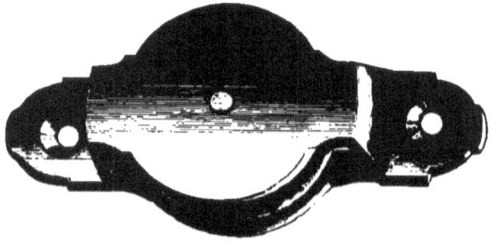

1¼ inch, Japanned	$0 62	per dozen.
1½ " "	75	"
2 "	90	"
2¼ "	1 40	"
2½ "	1 75	"
3	2 40	"
4	6 60	"

UPRIGHT PULLEYS.

1¾ inches, Japanned.. $0 60 per dozen.
2¼   "   "   .... 1 50   "

DUMB WAITER PULLEYS.

4-inch Wheel, Face 8¼ by 2¾, 4 Screw Holes, for 1-inch Rope.............. $7 50 per dozen.

CLOTHES-LINE PULLEYS.

No. 1, Japanned, 1¼ inch.. $1 00 per dozen.
 " 2, Galvanized,........................ .... 1 40   "

2¼ inches Japanned $1 00 per dozen.
2¼   1 20   "

SLIDING DOOR-SHEAVES.

1 1/2 inches
2
3
4
5

SLIDING DOOR RAIL.

Painted

CHAIN DOOR FASTENERS.

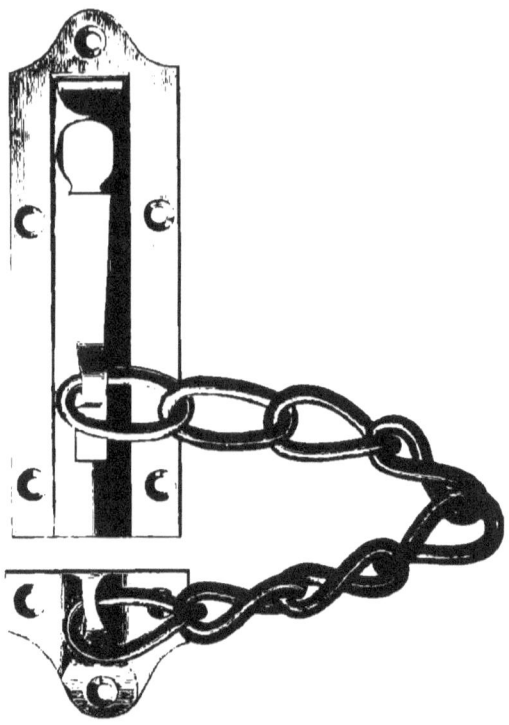

No. 4.

	Japanned	Gold Bronzed.	C. Plated.	Brass.
No. 1, 7½ inch,	$4 00	$6 00		$12 00 per doz.
" 2, 6½ "	3 12	5 20	$7 50	10 00 "
" 3, 5½ "	3 12	5 20	7 50	10 00 "
" 4, 4 "	2 50	4 50		7 50 "

CHAIN DOOR-FASTENER.

No. 5, 6 inches, Bronzed, with Bronzed Screws .... $3 75 per dozen.
" 6, "   Polished and Bronzed, with Bronzed Screws .... 6 00   "
" 7, "   Bronze Metal, with Brass Screws ....22 00   "

HEAVY BARREL BOLTS.
BRASS KNOBS.

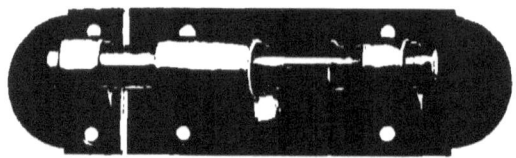

No. 5.

$0 75	$0 88	$1 12	$1 38	$1 62	$1 88 per dozen.
3	4	5	6	7	8 inch.

HEAVY TOWER BOLTS.

No. 10.

$0 62	$0 87	$1 13	$1 37	$1 63 per dozen.
4	5	6	7	8 inch.

HEAVY SHUTTER BOLTS.
BRASS KNOBS.

No. 15.

$0 75	$1 25	$1 75	$2 25	$2 75 per dozen.
5	6	8	10	12 inch.

Shutter Bolts--Wrought Iron.

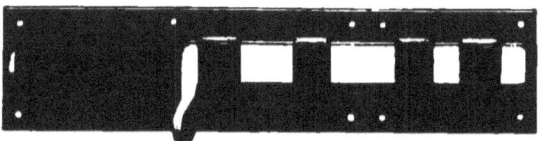

No 20--Japanned Plates, Polished Bolts

$2 75	$3 00	$3 38	$3 75	$4 25	$5 50	$7 25 per dozen.
6	7	8	9	10	12	14 inch.
					1x⅛	1x⅜ bolts.

No. 24--Japanned Plates, Galvanized Bolts

$2 75	$3 00	$3 38	$3 75	$4 25	$5 50	$7 25 per dozen.
6	7	8	9	10	12	14 inch.

No 28 A I Galvanized

$3 50	$4 00	$4 50	$5 00	$5 75	$6 50	$10 00 per dozen
6	7	8	9	10	12	14 inch.

Wrought-Iron Spring Bolts.

	3	4	4	4	5	3 in. square bolts
	4	5	6	7	8	10 inch.
No. 30, Japanned, $1 50	$1 75	$2 25	$2 75	$3 75	$5 25 per dozen.
" 35, Galvanized, 2 50	2 75	3 75	4 25	5 75	8 00	"

Wrought-Iron Necked Bolts.

¾	⅞ in. square bolts.
6	8 Inches.
No. 40, Japanned $2 50	$4 00 per dozen.
" 45, Galvanized 4 00	6 00 "

Barrel Bolts, with Bronzed Screws.

Nos. 60 and 65.

	3	4	5	6 Inches.
No. 60, Bronzed,...............	$2 20.	$2 60.	$3 10.	$3 75 per dozen.
" 65, Polished and Bronzed............	2 60.	3 00.	3 50.	4 25 "

Square Spring Bolts, with Bronzed Screws.

	3	4 Inches
No. 70, ...	$2 50	$2 75, per dozen.
" 75, ...	2 75	3 00 "

Bottom Bolts, Polished and Bronzed,

With Bronzed Screws.

No. 80.

6 inch... $5 00 per dozen
8 "   .... 6 00   "

SPRING BOLTS.—Cast Iron.

JAPANNED.

No. 50.

4	6	8 inch.
$0 75	$1 12	$1 88 per dozen.

Staples for Cast Spring Bolts.

For 4	6	8 inch.
$0 20	$0 25	$0 35 per dozen.

CHAIN BOLTS.

JAPANNED.

No. 55.

$2 35	$3 00	$4 00 per dozen.
4	6	8 inch.

THUMB LATCHES.
JAPANNED.

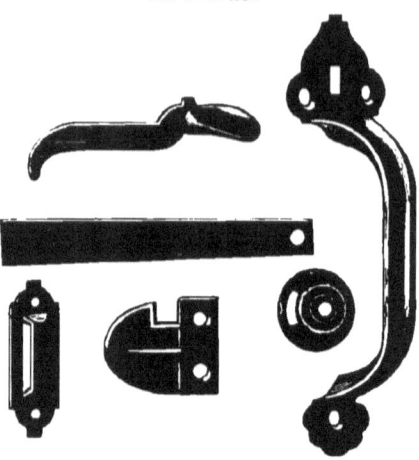

No. 1............$0 55 per dozen.   No. 3............$0 75 per dozen.
" 2............   65   "   " 4............   85   "
              24 DOZEN IN A CASE.

EXTRA HEAVY···Japanned.
No. 10............$0 45 per dozen.   No. 13............$0 75 per dozen.
" 11............   55   "   " 14............   85   "
" 12............   65   "   **24 DOZEN IN A CASE.**

GALVANIZED
No. 112..$1 25 per dozen.
" 114.. 1 50   "

Case Latches.

No. 7, Japanned..$1 00 per dozen.

DROP THUMB LATCHES.

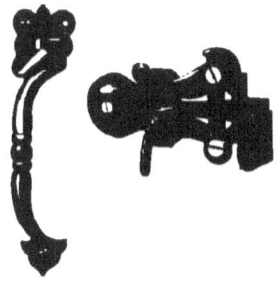

No. 1, Japanned..$0 80 per dozen.

24 DOZEN IN A CASE.

No. 2, Japanned..$0 85 per dozen.

24 DOZEN IN A CASE.

STORE DOOR LATCHES.

Nos. 1 and 11.

No. 1, Japanned .... $2 00 per dozen.
" 11, Galvanized .... 3 75 "

STORE DOOR LATCHES.

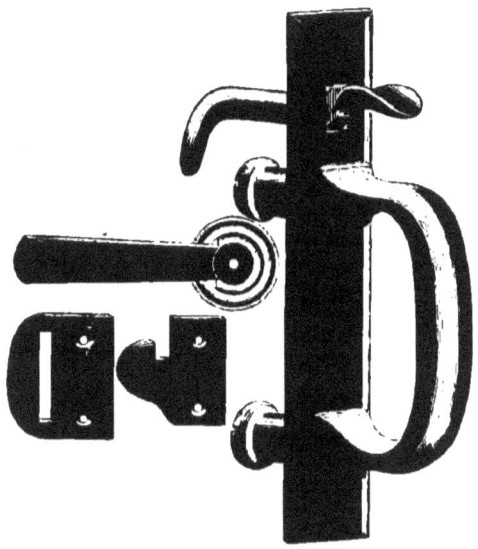

No. 2, Japanned...$3 75 per dozen.

Bronzed Store Door Latches,

With Bronzed Screws.

Nos. 3 and 13.

No. 3, Bronzed, ... $2 25 per dozen.
" 13, Polished and Bronzed, ... 4 00 "

THUMB LATCHES,

FOR BARN DOORS, GATES, &c.

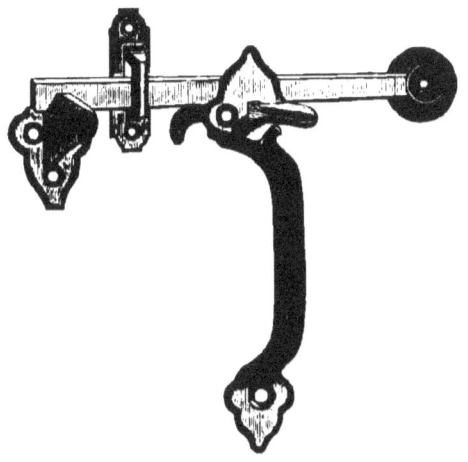

Nos. 1 and 11.

No. 1, Japanned	$2 63 per dozen.
" 11, Galvanized	4 00 "
" 2, Japanned, without Handle and Thumb-Piece	1 31 "

SAFETY SHUTTER-BOWER.

Malleable-Iron, Japanned	$6 00 per gross.
" " Tinned	8 00 "
Brass, Lacquered	16 00 "

SHUTTER STAYS,
With Wrought-Iron Shanks.

Nos. 3, 13 and 103.

No. 3, Japanned,...$7 50 per gross
" 103, " .... 6 75 "
" 13, Galvanized..13 50 "

With Malleable-Iron Shanks.

Nos. 23 and 33.

No. 23, Japanned ....$7 50 per gross.
" 33, Galvanized..13 50 "

Shutter-Stay Rosettes.

Japanned..................$1 75 per gross.   Galvanized ....$2 75 per gross.

SHUTTER STAYS.

No. 104, Japanned .... $7 50 per gross.
" 4, " .... 8 50 "
" 14, 2¼ inches, Japanned .... 10 00 "
" 24, 3 " " .... 10 50 "
" 34, 3½ " " .... 11 00 "
" 44, Galvanized .... 16 50 "
" 54, 2¼ inches, Galvanized .... 17 25 "
" 64, 3 " " .... 18 00 "
" 74, 3½ " " .... 18 75 "

No. 0, Half-Oval, Galvanized .... $27 00 per gross.
" 00, " Japanned .... 16 50 "
" 000, Flat, ⅜ by ⁵⁄₁₆, " .... 16 50 "
" 0000, " ⅜ by ⅜, " .... 28 00 "

Smith's Patent Wedge Shutter Stays,

TO PREVENT THE SHUTTER FROM RATTLING.

Nos. 7 and 17.

No. 7, Japanned .... $7 50 per gross.
" 17, Galvanized .... 13 50   "

Nos. 8 and 18.

No. 8, Japanned .... $8 50 per gross.
" 18, Galvanized .... 16 50   "

Inside and Outside Shutter Fasteners.

No. 3, for Brick .... $20 62 per gross.
" 4, for Frame.. 19 70 "

Inside Shutter Fastenings.

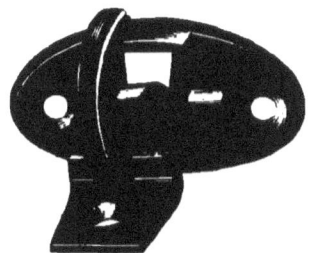

Nos. 2 and 12.

No. 2, Japanned..$4 75 per gross.
" 12, Galvanized... 6 00 "

SHUTTER HOOKS.

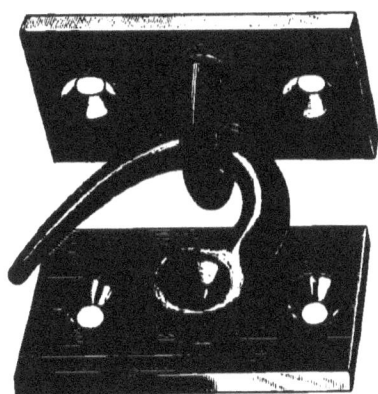

Nos. 1 and 11.

No. 1, Japanned..$9 00 per gross.
" 11, Galvanized... 12 50 "

WARDROBE HOOKS.

Nos. 3 and 13.

	JAPANNED.		BRONZED.
No. 1,	$0 50	No. 11,	$0 55 per gross.
" 2,	55	" 12,	60 "
" 3,	65	" 13,	72 "
" 4,	80	" 14,	88 "
" 5,	1 00	" 15,	1 10 "
" 400,	1 25		

Nos. 8, 18 and 28.

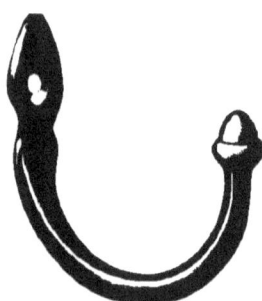

Nos. 10, 20 and 30.

JAPANNED.		BRONZED.		GALVANIZED.	
No. 8,	$0 75	No. 18,	$0 85	No. 28,	$1 25 per gross.
" 10,	1 35	" 20,	1 50	" 30,	2 25 "

WARDROBE HOOKS.

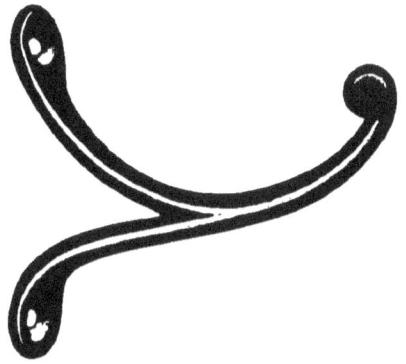

Nos. 60 and 65.

	JAPANNED.		BRONZED.
No. 50	$1 00	No. 55	$1 10 per gross.
" 60	1 25	" 65	1 38 "
" 70	1 75	" 75	1 75 "
" 500, Galvanized	1 25		
" 5000, Brass	5 00		

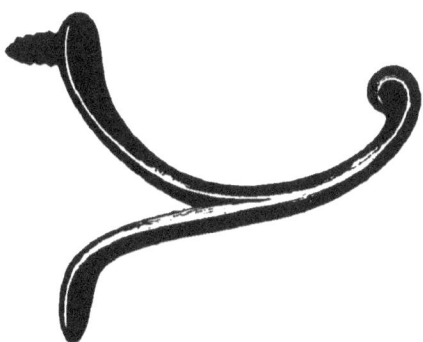

Nos. 40 and 42.

	JAPANNED.		BRONZED.
No. 35	$1 00	No. 37	$1 10 per gross.
" 40	1 25	" 42	1 38 "
" 45	1 50	" 48	1 75 "

HAT AND COAT HOOKS.

Nos. 75 and 80.

No. 75, Japanned .... $1 85 per gross.
" 80, Bronzed .... 2 05   "

12 GROSS IN A CASE.

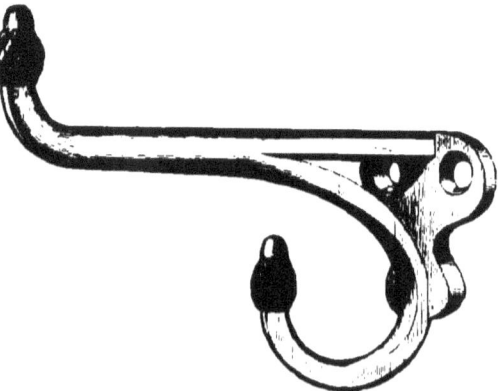

Nos. 4 and 14.

No. 4, Japanned .... $2 25 per gross.
" 14, Bronzed .... 2 45   "

12 GROSS IN A CASE.

HAT AND COAT HOOKS.

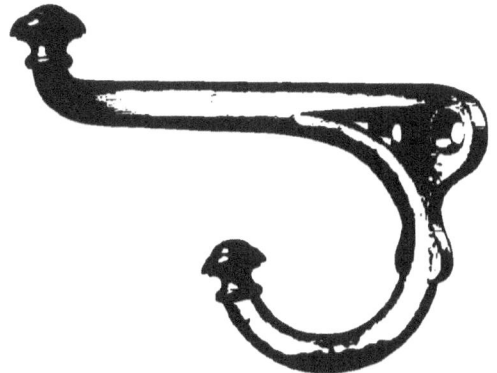

Nos. 104 and 114.

No. 104, Japanned .... $2 00 per gross.
" 114, Bronzed .... 2 20 "

12 GROSS IN A CASE.

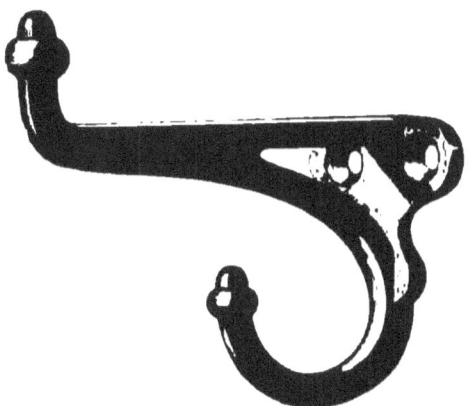

Nos. 7 and 17.

No. 7, Japanned .... $2 25 per gross.
" 17, Bronzed .... 2 45 "

12 GROSS IN A CASE.

HAT AND COAT HOOKS.

Nos. 11, 21 and 31.

No. 11, Japanned .... $1 80 per gross.
" 21, Bronzed .... 2 00 "
" 31, Galvanized .... 2 70 "

12 GROSS IN A CASE.

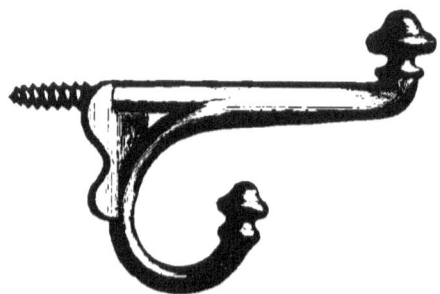

Nos. 12 and 22.

No. 12, Japanned .... $1 70 per gross.
" 22, Bronzed .... 1 90 "

12 GROSS IN A CASE.

HAT AND COAT HOOKS.

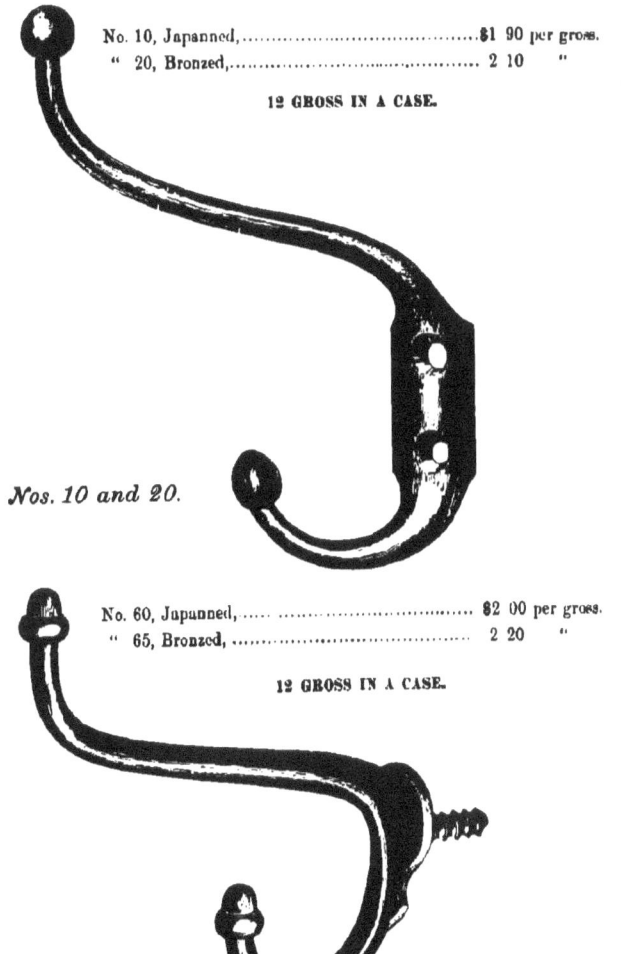

No. 10, Japanned,..................................$1 90 per gross.
" 20, Bronzed,..................................... 2 10   "

12 GROSS IN A CASE.

Nos. 10 and 20.

No. 60, Japanned,............................... $2 00 per gross.
" 65, Bronzed, ... 2 20   "

12 GROSS IN A CASE.

Nos. 60 and 65.

HAT AND COAT HOOKS.

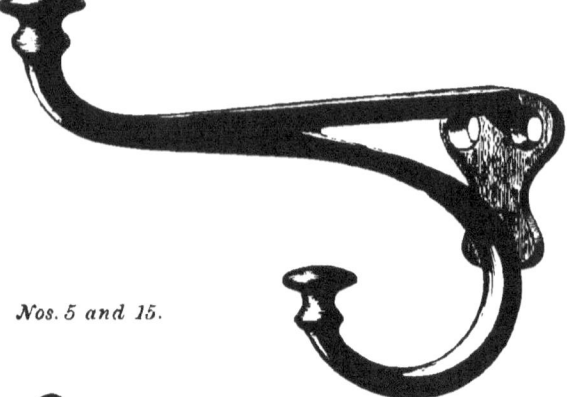

Nos. 5 and 15.

No. 5, Japanned............................$2 50 per gross.
" 15, Bronzed................................ 2 70   "

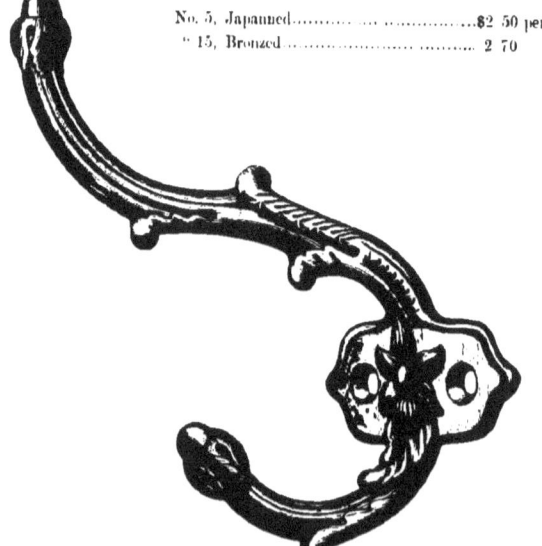

Nos. 81, 85 and 86.

No. 81, Japanned..$3 12 per gross.
" 85, Bronzed... 3 43   "
" 86, Solid Bronze...................................... 4 00 per dozen.

HAT AND COAT HOOKS.

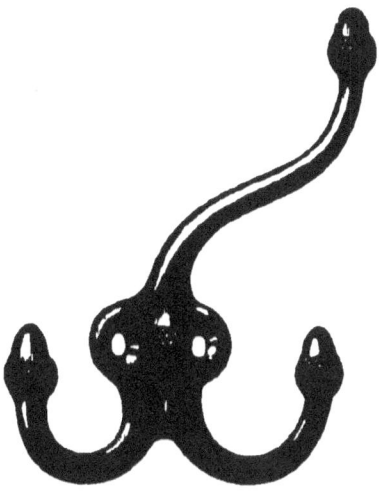

No. 180, Japanned............ $2.25 per gross
"   185, Bronzed............   2.50   "

GUM SPRING HOOKS.

Japanned.. $1.00 per gross pairs.

SCHOOL-HOUSE HOOKS.

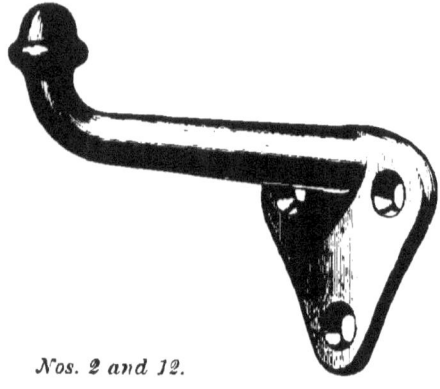

Nos. 2 and 12.

No. 2, Japanned .... $3 00 per gross
" 12, Bronzed .... 3 30   "

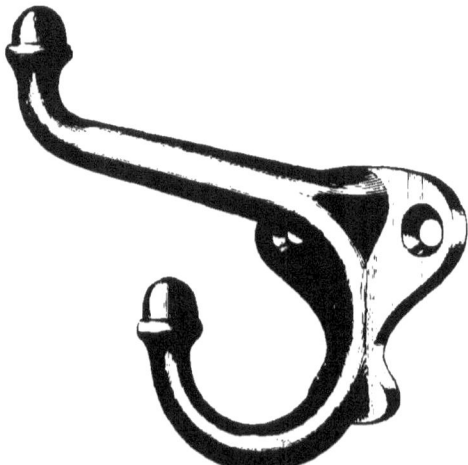

Nos. 1 and 11.

No. 1, Japanned .... $4 25 per gross
" 11, Bronzed .... 4 75   "

HEAD-BOARD HOOKS AND EYES.

Nos. 2 and 4.

	JAPANNED.	GOLD BRONZED.	BRASS.
No. 2, Malleable Iron	$1 56	$2 50	$4 00 per dozen sets.
" 4, Cast Iron	75		" "

Nos. 1 and 3.

	JAPANNED OR COPPER BRONZED.	GOLD BRONZED.	BRASS.
No. 1, Malleable Iron	$2 50	$3 75	$7 50 per dozen sets.
" 3, Cast Iron	1 50		" "

HARNESS HOOKS.

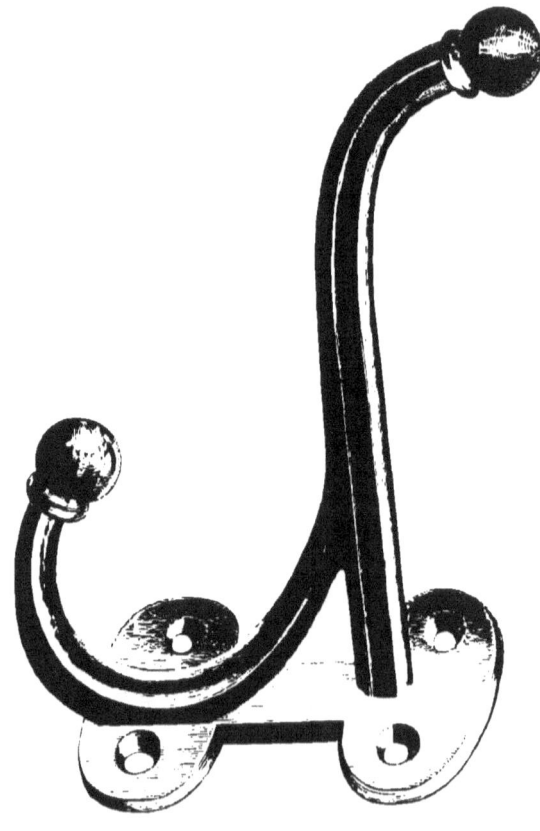

Nos. 0, 1, 2, 4 and 5.

HARNESS HOOKS.

No. 3.

	JAPANNED.
No. 0, 10½ inches	$4 30 per dozen.
" 1, 6 "	1 00 "
" 2, 4 "	65 "
" 3, 8 "	1 10 "
" 4, 8½ "	2 00 "
" 5, 7 "	1 20 "

CEILING HOOKS.

No. 1.
JAPANNED.
$2 20

No. 11.
BRONZED.
$2 45

No. 21.
GOLD BRONZED.
$4 00 per gross.

12 GROSS IN A CASE.

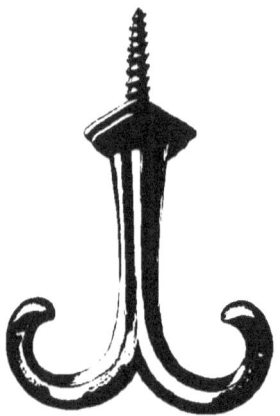

No. 2.
JAPANNED.
$1 60

No. 12.
BRONZED.
$1 80 per gross.

12 GROSS IN A CASE.

CEILING HOOKS.

Nos. 120 and 135.

No. 120, Japanned..$1 25 per gross.
" 135, Bronzed.. 1 45 "

12 GROSS IN A CASE.

No. 10, Japanned........................... $7 00 per gross.

CLOTHES-LINE HOOKS.

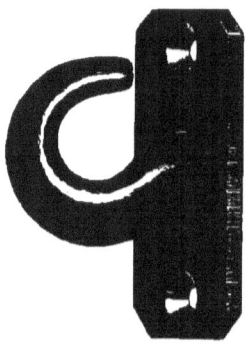

Nos. 1 and 11.

No. 1, Japanned .... $5 50 per gross
" 11, Galvanized .... 10 00   "

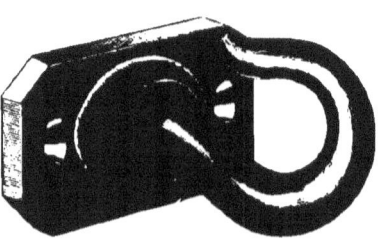

Nos. 20 and 25.

No. 20, Japanned .... $6 00 per gross.
" 25, Galvanized .... 10 50   "

CLOTHES-LINE HOOKS.

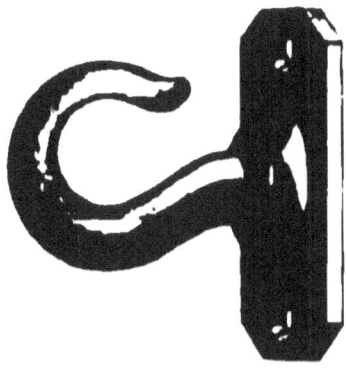

Nos. 2 and 12.

No. 2, Japanned .... $6.00 per gross
" 12, Galvanized .... 10.40   "

Nos. 2½ and 12½.

No. 2½, Japanned .... $7.40 per gross
" 12½, Galvanized .... 14.00   "

CLOTHES-LINE HOOKS.

	JAPANNED.	GALVANIZED.
3½ inch,	$3 00.	$4 00 per gross.

Nos. 1 and 11.

No. 1, Japanned, ... $5 00 per gross.
" 11, Galvanized, ... 8 50 "

CLOTHES-LINE HOOKS.

Nos. 3 and 13.

No. 3, Japanned..$10 00 per gross.
" 13, Galvanized............................... 18 00 "

Bird-Cage Hooks.

No. 1, 9 Inches, Japanned $1 50 per dozen
" 2, 8 "   "   1 25   "
" 3, 8 "   "   (to screw on)   1 25
" 11, 9 "   Green-and-Gold Bronzed   2 00
" 12, 8 "   "   "   1 60   "
" 13, 8 "   "   "   (to screw on)   1 60   "

BIRD CAGE HOOKS.

Nos. 7 and 17.

No. 7, Dark Bronzed... $2 25 per dozen.
" 17, Polished and Bronzed... 2 50 "

Nos. 5 and 15.

No. 5, Green-and-Gold Bronzed... $2 00 per dozen.
" 15, Galvanized .... 3 00 "
" 6, 12 inch, Green-and-Gold Bronzed............................. 4 00 "
" 16, " Galvanized .... 5 00 "

Hat Rack Plates.

Hat-Rack Hooks.

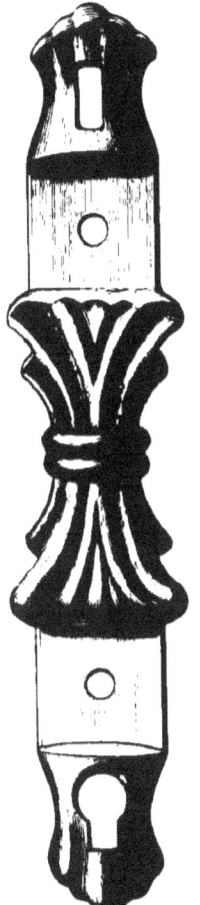

Bronzed ....$2 00 per gross.

Japanned ....$4 00 per gross.

LAMP HOOKS.

	1¼	1½	1¾	2¼	2½ inches.
	$2 00	$2 65	$3 30	$5 00	$6 56 per gross.
Japanned	No. 1	2	3	4	5

Picture or Looking-Glass Hooks

$1 25	$1 50	$2 00	$2 50 per gross.
2½	3	3½	4½ inches.

AWNING HOOKS.

2½ inches .... $1 00 per gross.   Galvanized .... $1 40 per gross.

CHEST HANDLES.

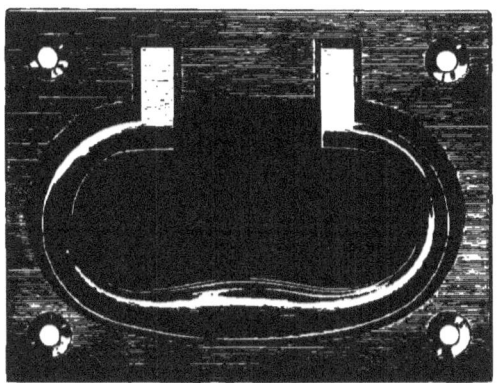

FLUSH.

	JAPANNED.
No. 1, 2¼ by 3 inches	$1 75 per dozen pairs.
" 2, 2¾ by 3½ "	2 25 " "
" 3, 3½ by 4¼ "	5 00 " "
" 4, 4¼ by 5¼ "	5 50 " "

Wrought Chest Handles.

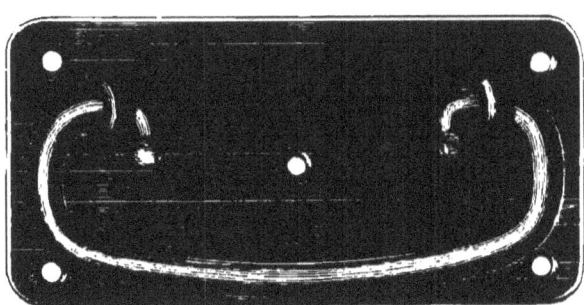

No. 2, 4¼ by 2¼ inches	$2 30 per dozen pairs.
" 3, 4¼ by 2¼ "	2 80 " "

CHEST HANDLES.

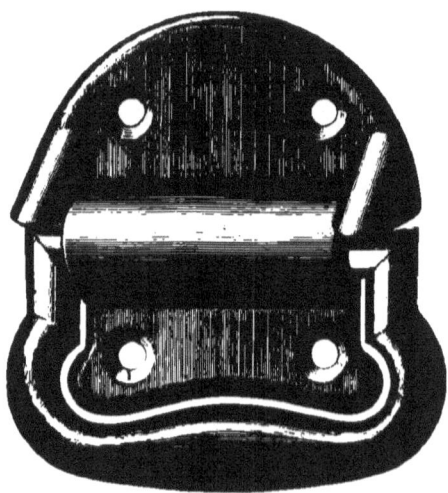

Nos. 1871 and 2871.

No. 1871, Japanned .... $2 00 per dozen pairs.
 " 1872,   "   .... 3 50   "   "
 " 1873,   "   .... 5 00   "   "
 " 2871, Bronzed .... 2 20   "   "
 " 2872,   "   .... 2 85   "   "
 " 2873,   "   .... 5 50   "   "
 " 1875,   "   with Oval Plates, for Tubs, Japanned .... 4 50   "   "
 " 2875,   "   "   "   "   Tinned .... 7 50   "   "
 " 3875,   "   "   "   "   Galvanized .... 7 50   "   "
 " 4875,   "   "   "   " Malleable Iron, Galvaniz'd 9 00 "   "

CHEST HANDLES.

Nos. 11 and 21.

No. 10, Japanned	$1 12	per dozen pairs.
" 11, "	1 50	"	"
" 20, Bronzed	1 25	"	"
" 21, "	1 65	"	"

DRAWER PULLS.

Nos. 58, 59 and 60.

No. 58, Japanned	$3 50 per gross.
" 59, Dark Bronzed, with Screws	4 00 "
" 60, Polished and Dark Bronzed, with Screws	5 50 "

Nos. 63, 64 and 65.

No. 63, Japanned	$4 00 per gross.
" 64, Dark Bronzed, with Screws	4 50 "
" 65, Polished and Dark Bronzed, with Screws	6 75 "

Nos. 68, 69 and 70.

No. 68, Japanned	$4 50 per gross.
" 69, Dark Bronzed, with Screws	5 00 "
" 70, Polished and Dark Bronzed, with Screws	8 00 "

DRAWER PULLS.

Nos. 10 and 20.

No. 10, Japanned .... $2 16 per gross.
" 20, Copper Bronzed .... 2 40 "

Nos. 8 and 18.

No. 8, Japanned .... $2 60 per gross.
" 18, Copper Bronzed .... 2 85 "

Nos. 50, 51 and 52.

No. 50, Japanned .... $3 75 per gross.
" 51, Copper Bronzed .... 4 00 "
" 52, Gold Bronzed .... 6 00 "

DRAWER PULLS.

Nos. 7 and 17.

No. 7, Japanned .... $2 40 per gross.
" 17, Copper Bronzed .... 2 60   "

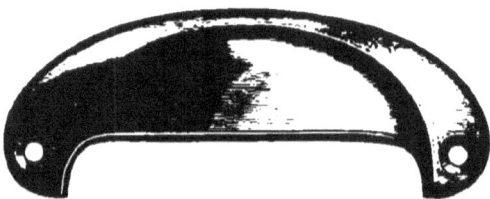

Nos. 6 and 16.

No. 6, Japanned .... $2 60 per gross.
" 16, Copper Bronzed .... 2 85   "

Nos. 1, 11 and 111.

No. 1, Japanned .... $3 75 per gross.
" 11, Copper Bronzed .... 4 00   "
" 111, Gold Bronzed .... 5 00   "

DRAWER PULLS.

Nos. 3, 13 and 113.

No. 3, Japanned .... $3 75 per gross.
" 13, Copper Bronzed .... 4 00 "
" 113, Gold Bronzed .... 5 00 "

Nos. 4 and 14.

No. 4, Japanned .... $3 75 per gross.
" 14, Copper Bronzed .... 4 00 "

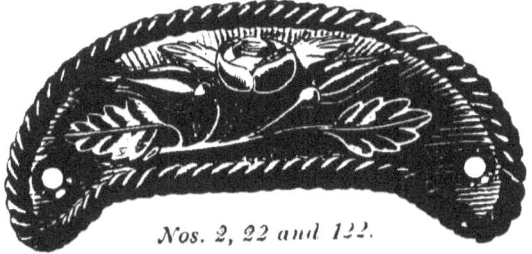

Nos. 2, 22 and 122.

No. 2, Japanned .... $3 75 per gross.
" 22, Copper Bronzed .... 4 00 "
" 122, Gold Bronzed .... 6 00 "

Bronzed Cupboard Catches,

WITH BRONZED SCREWS

No. 29, Bronzed, with Bronze-Metal Knobs .... $9 00 per gross.
" 30, Polished and Bronzed, with Bronze-Metal Knobs .... 13 00 "
" 34, Bronzed, with Porcelain Knobs .... 9 00 "
" 35, Polished and Bronzed, with Porcelain Knobs .... 13 00 "

Bronzed French Window Catches,

WITH BRONZED SCREWS.

No. 20, 1¼ inches, Polished and Bronzed, with Bronze-Metal Knobs......... $10 00 per gross.
" 25, 1¼ " " " with Porcelain Knobs............. 10 00 "

CUPBOARD CATCHES.

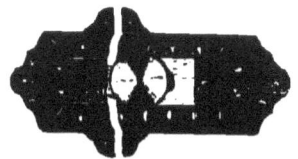

Half-size Cut of Nos 375 and 376.

No. 375, Japanned, Brass Knobs...$12 50 per gross.
" 376, French Bronzed, Brass Knobs............................... 16 00 "

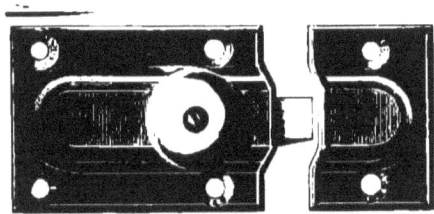

Nos. 15 and 16.

No. 15, Japanned, Porcelain Knobs..$6 25 per gross.
" 16, Bronzed, " .... 6 25 "

Nos. 10 and 11.

No. 10, Japanned, Porcelain Knobs..$7 25 per gross.
" 11, Bronzed, " .... 7 25 "

SASH FASTENERS.

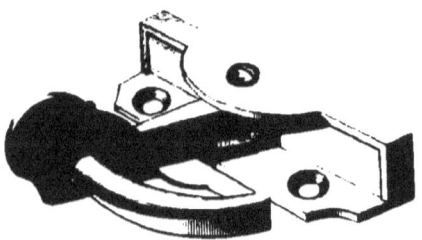

Nos. 1 and 2.

No. 1, Japanned ...... $5 00 per gross.
" 2, Bronzed ... 6 00 "

Nos. 11, 12 and 21.

No. 11, Japanned, Porcelain Knob .... $12 00 per gross
 12, Bronzed, " " .... 13 00 "
 21, Polished and Bronzed, Porcelain Knob ..... 15 00 "

SASH FASTENERS.

No. 31, Brass, Porcelain Knob .... $37 00 per gross.

No. 3, Bronzed......... .... $7 00 per gross.
" 13, Polished and Bronzed .... 8 00 "

CUP CUPBOARD-KNOBS.

No. 2, Japanned ....$1 55 per gross.

SHUTTER KNOBS.

No. 5, Bronzed ....$4 00 per gross.
" 10, Polished and Bronzed .... 4 75   "

SHUTTER BARS.

2¼ inch, No. 1, Bronzed, with Bronzed Screws .... $5 40 per gross.
3   "   "   1,   "   "   "   " .... 6 00   "
2¼ "   "   2, Polished and Bronzed, with Bronzed Screws .... 6 00   "
3   "   "   2,   "   "   "   "   "   " .... 6 75   "

2¼ inch Brass, Polished and Lacquered.................................$21 00 per gross

SASH FASTENERS.

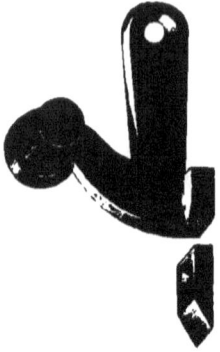

No. 20, Japanned .... $1 75 per gross.

No. 10, Bronzed .... $1 20 per gross.

Y SASH DROPS.

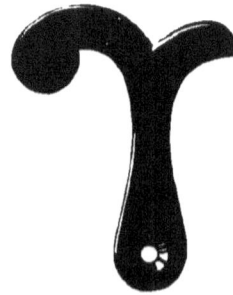

Japanned .... $1 10 per gross.

SASH LIFTS.

Nos. 5, 10 and 110.

No.   5, Bronzed, with Bronzed Screws .... $4 00 per gross.
"   10, Polished and Bronzed, with Bronzed Screws........................... 4 35   "
"   110, Bronze Metal, with Brass Screws..20 00   "

Nos. 15 and 115.

No. 15, Polished and Bronzed, with Bronzed Screws .... $7 75 per gross.
"   115, Bronze Metal, with Brass Screws   46 00   "

   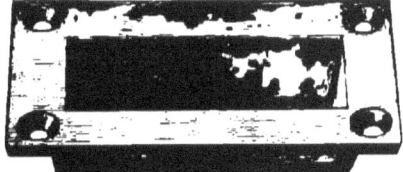

No. 4.   *No. 3.*

	JAPANNED.	GOLD BRONZED.
No. 3	$6 00	$7 00 per gross.
" 4	2 50	3 00 "

STUBS AND PLATES.

 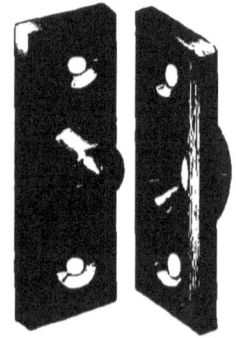

No. 1. *No. 2.*
No. 1, Japanned .... $2 75 per gross.   No. 2, Japanned .... $3 25 per gross.

TRANSOM PLATES.

No. 1.
No. 1, Japanned ....$3 90 per gross.   No. 2, Japanned.. ....$7 50 per gross.

SHUTTER LIFTS

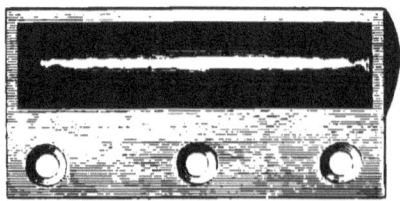

No. 2, Japanned ...   .$3 00 per gross.

SHUTTER SCREWS.

	1½	1¾	2	2¼	2½	2¾	3 inches.	
Japanned								$8 00 per gross.

SASH ROLLERS.

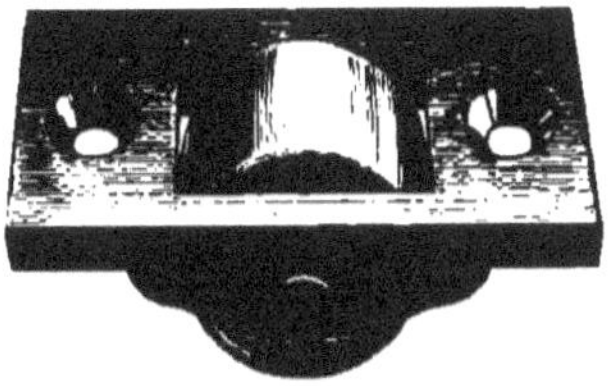

	WIDTH OF PLATE.	
No. 1, Japanned, Polished Wheels	⅝ inch.	$3 25 per gross.
" 2, " " "	¾ "	3 50 "
" 3, " " "	⅞ "	4 00 "
" 4, " " "	1 "	4 75 "
" 5, " " "	1¼ "	5 50 "
" 6, " " "	1½ "	6 50 "

CHEST ROLLERS.

Japanned, Polished Wheels .... $2 00 per dozen.

Malleable-Iron Staples, for Wire Fence.

90 cents per gross.

HINGE HASPS.

No. 1.

	JAPANNED.
8 inches	$3 00 per dozen.
10 "	3 50 "

No. 2.

	JAPANNED.
6 inches	$3 00 per dozen.
8 "	3 75 "
10 "	5 00 "

SAW RODS.

No. 2 Wire, 19, 20 inches..$12 50 per gross.

DOOR KNOCKERS.

Nos. 1 and 3. *No. 2.*

	JAPANNED.	BRONZED.	BRASS.	GALVANIZED.
No. 1	$13 50	$17 50		$18 75 per dozen.
" 2	4 00	6 00	$11 00	6 00 "
" 3	8 00	12 00		12 00 "

DOOR BUTTONS.

	1¼	1½	1¾	2	2¼	2½	3 inches.
Japanned	$0 40	$0 50	$0 62	$0 80	$1 00	$1 40	$3 00 per gross.
Galvanized				1 10	1 50	2 10	4 50 "
Brass				4 00			"

ON PLATES.

	JAPANNED.	GALVANIZED.	BRASS.	
1 inch	$2 25			per gross.
1½ "	2 63			"
2 "	3 00	$4 75	$13 50	"

VENTILATORS.

	JAPANNED.
4 inches	$2 00 per dozen.
6 "	3 00 "

STAY NAILS.

		GALVANIZED.
6 inches	$4 70	$5 75 per gross.
7 "	5 50	7 50 "

IRON PLUMB-BOBS.

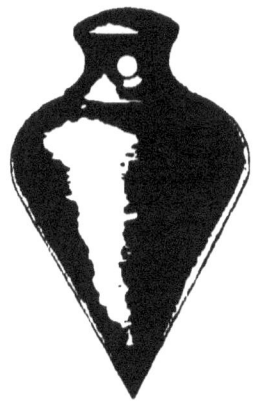

JAPANNED

No. 1, 7¼ lbs	$1 06 per dozen.	No. 3, 13½ lbs	$1 44 per dozen
" 2, 9½ lbs	1 25 "	" 4, 18 lbs	2 00 "

SHEAVE WHEELS—TURNED.

3 inches	$2 81 per dozen.	6 inches, No. 1	$6 25 per dozen.
4 "	3 75 "	6 " " 2	6 87 "
5 " No. 1	5 31 "	6 " " 3	7 50 "
5 " " 2	6 25 "	6 " " 4	9 00 "

DRAWER PULLS.

Nos. 9 and 19.

No. 9, Japanned .... $18 75 per gross.
" 19, Bronzed .... 27 00   "

DOOR PULLS.

No. 5, Japanned .... $4 00 per gross.
" 7, Bronzed .... 4 50   "

TABLE-LEAF SUPPORTS.

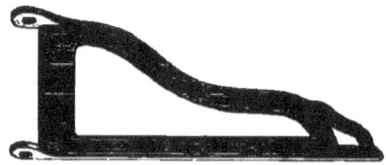

12 inches .... $1 50 per dozen.

CLOTH CLAMPS.

1 inch, Japanned, with Steel Set Screws .... $1.00 per dozen.

QUILTING-FRAME CLAMPS.

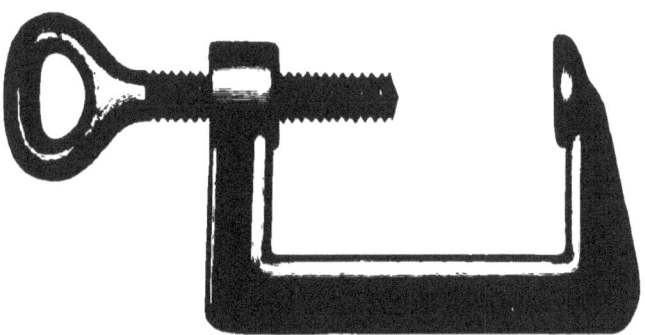

No. 00, opens 2¼ inches, Japanned .... $0.70 per dozen.

OAR-LOCKS.
MALLEABLE IRON.

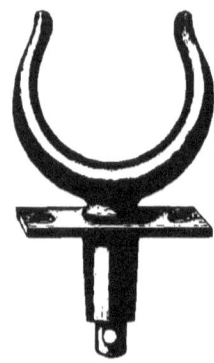

	No. 2.	3	3½
Galvanized	$5 50	$8 00	$14 00 per dozen pairs.
Not "	4 00	6 00	10 00 " "

	No. 1.	1½	4
Galvanized	$5 50	$7 00	$10 00 per dozen pairs.
Not "	4 00	5 00	7 20 " "

RUDDER BRACES--Galvanized.

MALLEABLE IRON.

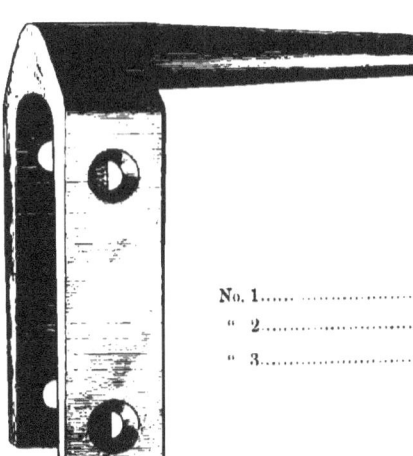

No. 1 .... $1 75 per dozen.
" 2 .... 2 25   "
" 3 .... 3 00   "

No. 1.

CLEATS--Malleable Iron.

GALVANIZED.

Nos. 6 and 7.

No. 6, 4¼ inches .... $0 60 per dozen.
"   7, 6¼   "   .... 1 20   "

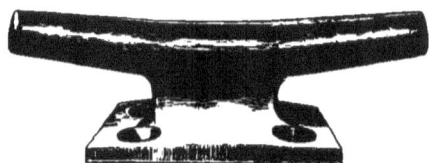

Nos. 1, 2 and 3.

No. 1, 2 inches .... $1 00 per dozen.
"   2, 3¼   "   .... 1 25   "
"   3, 3¾   "   .... 1 90   "

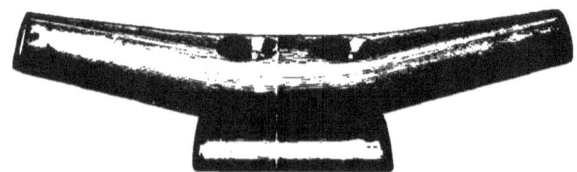

Nos. 4 and 5.

No. 4, 4½ inches .... $1 90 per dozen.
"   5, 5¼   "   .... 2 50   "

TACKLE BLOCKS.

MALLEABLE IRON.

GALVANIZED

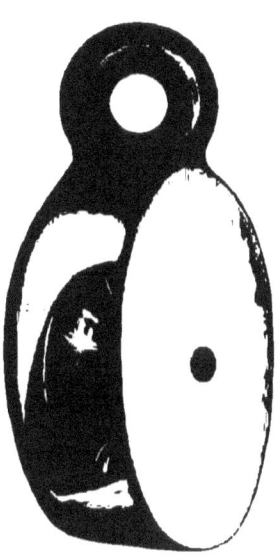

No. 3.

	For	¼	⅜	½	⅝	¾	⅞	1 inch Rope
		1	1¼	1½	1¾	2¼	3	4 inch Wheel
	Nos. 0	1	1½	2	3	5	6	7
1 Eye		$1 00	$1 20	$1 60	$2 00	$2 80	$6 50	$7 50	$15 00 per dozen
2 Eye,	Nos. 10	11	11½	12	13			
		$1 10	$1 30	$1 75	$2 15	$3 00		
1 Eye, Double,	Nos. 21	21½	22	23				
		$2 40	$3 20	$4 00	$5 50			
Hook and Eye				Nos. 32	33	35	36	37
				$2 15	$3 00	$7 00	$8 00	$16 00
" " Double					Nos. 45	46	47	
					$11 00	$12 00	$24 00	

THIMBLES--Malleable Iron.

GALVANIZED.

$0 25	$0 35	$0 40	$0 50	$0 55	$0 65	$0 75	$0 90	$1 05	$1 20 per dozen.
⅞	1	1⅛	1¼	1½	2	2¼	2½	2¾	3 inches.

AWNING-FRAME PLATES.

MALLEABLE IRON—GALVANIZED.

No. 1 .... $0 80 per dozen.

No. 2 .... $1 00 per dozen.

HATCH ROPE-EYES.

⅜ inch ....$0 75 per dozen.
2¼ " .... 1 25   "

RINGS.
MALLEABLE IRON—GALVANIZED.

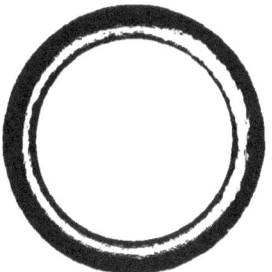

⅝	¾	⅞	1	1¼ inches.
$0 70	$0 80	$0 90	$1 10	$1 40 per gross

1¼ inches .... Nos. 4   6   8
                                      $1 70 $1 60 $1 50
1½ "   .... Nos. 1   3   6
                                      $2 75 $2 00 $1 60 per gross
1¾ "   .... Nos. 0   1   2
                                      $3 50 $3 25 $3 00 "
2   "   .... No. 0, $4 90 per gross.
2¼ "   ....   " $6 50   "
2½ "   ....   "   7 25   "
3   "   ....   "   8 50   "

PLATE CASTERS.

BRONZED.

IRON.

	Nos.	1	2	3	4	5	6	7	
A.	All Iron	$0 10	$0 11	$0 12	$0 15	$0 17	$0 20	$0 28	per set
B.	Brass Wheel	20	25	30	36	45	57	75	"
C.	Lignum-Vitæ Wheel	14	15	18	22	26	30	35	"
D.	Porcelain Wheel	12	13	15	18	20	24	28	"

BRASS.

H.	All Brass	37	48	56	65	80	95		"
I.	Lignum-Vitæ Wheel	32	35	43	55	65	75		"
J.	Porcelain Wheel	32	35	43	55	65	75		"

PIANO-FORTE CASTERS.

		1¼	1½ inches.
K.	Iron, Polished Wheels	$0 50	$0 60 per set.
L.	Iron, Lignum-Vitæ Wheels	55	65 "

SOCKET CASTERS.

	⅞	1	1¼	1⅜	1½	1⅝ inches.
M. Brass, Lignum-Vitæ Wheel	$0 33	$0 38	$0 50	$0 60	$0 70	$0 80 per set.
N. " Porcelain Wheel	33	38	50	60	70	80 "
O. All Brass	42	53	64	75	85	1 05 "

FRENCH CASTERS.

	Nos.	1	2	3	4
All Iron		$0 13	$0 14	$0 16	$0 18 per set.
Iron, Lignum-Vitæ Wheel		16	18	22	26 "
" Porcelain Wheel		16	18	22	26 "
Brass, Lignum-Vitæ Wheel		32	36	40	50 "

BED CASTERS.
BRONZED.

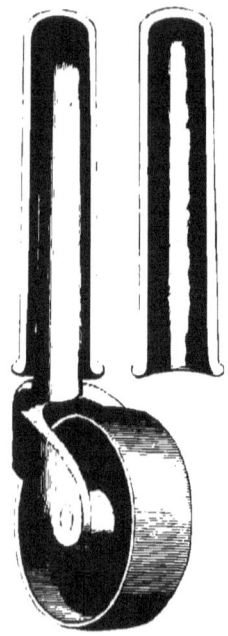

		Nos. 0	1	2	1	2	3	
		1½	1½	1½	2	2	2	2¼ inches.
Q.	All Iron	10½	12	13	16	18	20	40 cts. per set.
R.	Dog-Wood Wheel		15	16	18	20	25	50 "
S.	Lignum-Vitæ Wheel		19	22	25	28	35	75 "
U.	Porcelain Wheel		19	22	25	28	35	"

GLOBE WHEEL.

		1½	2 inches.
V.	All Iron		$0 35 per set.
W.	Lignum-Vitæ Wheel	33	45 "
X.	Porcelain Wheel	33	45 "

BRACKET BED CASTERS.
BRONZED

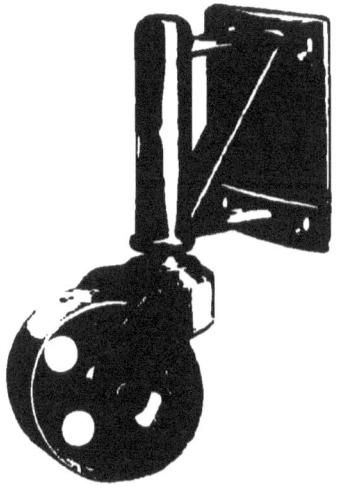

3 inches.

Y. All Iron................................ 40 40 per set
Z. Lignum Vitæ Wheel............. 90 "
ZZ. Dog-Wood Wheel................ 80

Sewing-Machine Casters.

Lignum-Vitæ Wheels   40 40 per set

BOX CASTERS.

3 inches ....$1 20 per set.
4   "   .... 1 60   "

TRUCK WHEELS.

5	6	7 inches.
1	1¼	1½ inch Face.
$4 00	$6 00	$8 00 per dozen.

BED KEYS.

No. 3.   *Nos. 4 and 14.*

	JAPANNED.
No. 4	$1 25 per dozen.
" 3, Malleable	1 75 "
" 14, "	1 87 "

BEDSTEAD FASTENERS.

No. 2, 1½ lbs., and No. 7, 1½ lbs. to set.

No. 2, Papered	80	13 per set.
" 7, "		12 "
Loose, in Barrels		06 per lb.
" in Kegs		06½ "

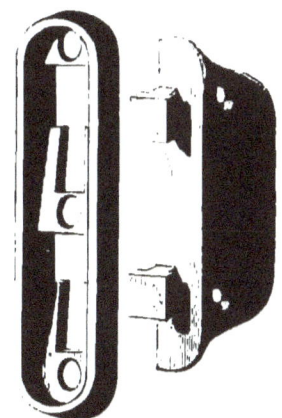

No. 3, 2½ lbs., and No. 10, 2½ lbs. to set.

No. 3, Papered	80	18 per set.
" 10, "		20 "
Loose, in Barrels		06 per lb.
" in Kegs		06½ "

BEDSTEAD FASTENERS.

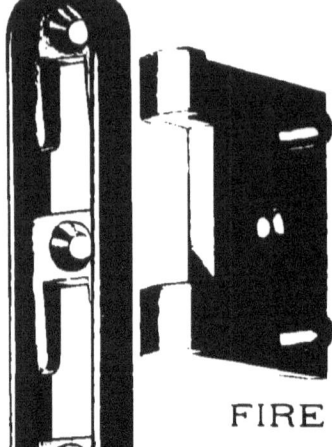

No. 20.
3½ lbs. to Set.

Papered	$0 24 per set.
Loose, in Barrels	06 per lb.
" Kegs	06½ "

FIRE DETECTORS.

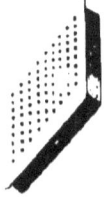

Bronzed ....$8 75 per dozen.

LETTER-BOX PLATES.

Japanned	$3 50 per dozen.
Gold-Bronzed	4 75 "
Brass	10 00 "

CARR, CRAWLEY & DEVLIN'S CATALOGUE.

THE "GEM"
TOBACCO CUTTER.

(PATENT PENDING)

No. 5.

This Tobacco Cutter is constructed upon a principle which gives the blade a draw cut of 2¼ inches, thereby slicing the tobacco with a smooth, clean cut. Tobacco 1¼ inches thick, sliced with but little pressure.

1 Dozen in a Case...$18.00 per doz.

[BLANK PAGE]

TOBACCO CUTTERS.

No. 2.

No. 3.

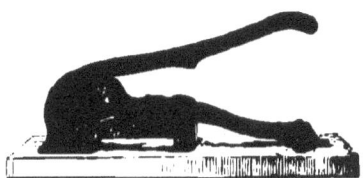

No. 4.

No. 2	$15 00 per dozen
" 3	13 00 "
" 4	14 00 "

1 DOZEN IN A CASE.

Window-Shade Brackets.

BRONZED

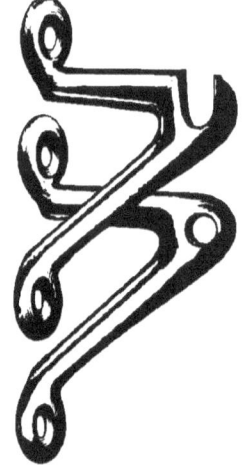

Nos. 1 and 2.   *No. 5.*

No. 1...... .... $2 75 per gross pairs.
" 2   .... 3 00   "   "
" 5   .... 4 00   "   "

10 GROSS IN A CASE.

WINDOW SHADE BRACKETS.
BRONZED.

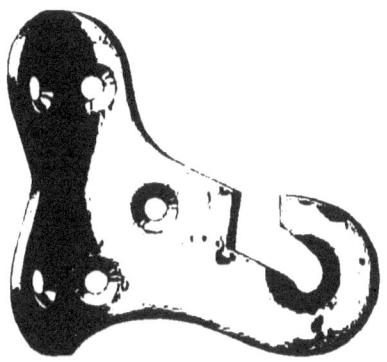

No. 10............................ .... $13 50 per gross pairs.

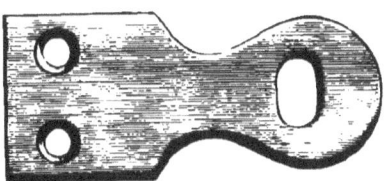

No. 15.. $9 00 per gross pairs.

Window-Shade Roller Ends.
BRONZED.

Nos. 2 and 12.

No. 2, without Eyes .... $3 70 per gross.
" 12, with   "   .... 4 00   "

No. 5.

No. 5, with Eyes.......   .... $6 25 per gross.

10 GROSS IN A CASE.

SHADE-CORD HOLDER.

BRONZED.

$2 50 per gross.

Roller-Ends or Spools, for Store Shades.

No. 10, 2¼ inches Diameter .... $15 00 per gross.
" 15, 3   "   "   .... 18 00   "

WINDOW-SHADE RACKS.

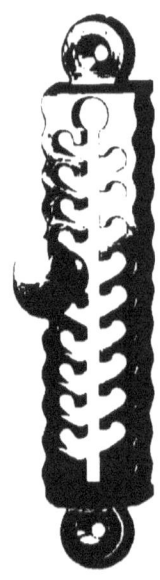

No. 4.   No. 5.

No. 4 Lacquered $3.75 per gross.
   "   5.50   "

SOAP CUPS.

3 by 5 Inches.

Galvanized..$1 25 per dozen.

SPITTOONS.

BRONZED.

Nos. 6, 7 and 8.

No. 6, 10 inches...$15 00 per dozen.
" 7, 12 " .... 20 00 "
" 8, 15 " .... 40 00 "

FOOT SCRAPERS.

No. 2.

No. 3.

No. 10.

No. 4.

No. 8.

No. 7.

	JAPANNED.	GALVANIZED.
No. 2	$0 50	$1 75 per dozen.
" 3	1 00	2 00 "
" 4	1 75	3 50 "
" 7	4 25	8 00 "
" 8	4 25	8 00 "
" 10	1 30	2 60 "

FOOT SCRAPERS.

No. 9.

No. 13.   *No. 11.*

	NOT JAPANNED.	JAPANNED.	BRONZED.	GALVANIZED
No. 9	$4 25	$5 00		$8 00 per dozen.
" 11			$12 00	"
" 12		6 00		"
" 13			30 00	"

GRINDSTONE FIXTURES.

No. 1.

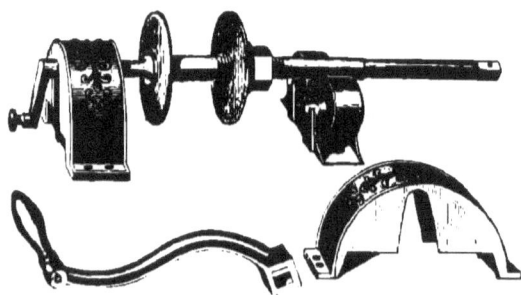

Nos. 2, 3 and 4.

	SIZE OF WHEELS ON FACE	LENGTH OF SHAFT.	SIZE OF STONE		
No. 1,	2 inch.	15 inch	3 inch.	$8 00 per dozen sets.	
" 2,	2 "	18 "	3 "	15 00	" "
" 3,	2 "	20 "	3½ "	17 00	" "
" 4,	1 "	19 "	4 "	20 00	" "
" 5,	1½ "	19 " very heavy	4½ "	24 00	" "
" 6,	1½ "	26 " " "	6 "	30 00	" "

1-2 DOZEN SETS IN A CASE.

FRICTION ROLLERS.

No. 1, for No. 1 and 2 Shafts				$4 25	per dozen sets.	
" 2	"	3	"	6 00	"	"
" 3,	"	4	"	7 00	"	"
" 4,	"	5 " 6	"	10 00	"	"

GARDEN HOES.

3 Prong, Steel Blade, Handled........................... $4 00 per dozen.
4   "   "   "   .... 4 50   "
3 " Solid "   "   .... 4 00   "
Floral Hoes,   "   .... 7 00 per gross.

POTATOE HOES.

4 Prong, Handled................................... $4 00 per dozen.

MALLEABLE IRON RAKES.
JAPANNED.

6 Teeth, Handled .... $3 75 per dozen.
8   "   "   .... 4 50   "
10 "   "   .... 5 00   "
12 "   "   .... 5 75   "
14 "   "   .... 6 25   "

GRIDIRONS.

| $4 00 | $4 50 | $5 00 | $6 00 | $7 00 per dozen. |
| 6 | 7 | 8 | 10 | 12 bars. |

CORK PRESSERS.

	JAPANNED.	BRONZED.
No. 2	$3 50	$4 50 per dozen.
" 3	3 25	4 25 "

SADIRON STANDS.

No. 9.

No. 4.

No. 10.

No. 8.

No. 2.

No. 2, 9 inches	$10 00	per gross.
" 4, 7¼ "	9 00	"
" 8, 9½ "	13 00	"
" 9, 8 "	9 00	"
" 10, 9¼ "	20 00	"

COFFEE-POT STANDS.

5½ Inches.

Japanned	$9 60	per gross.
Bronzed	10 60	"

Townsend's Patent Lemon-Squeezers.

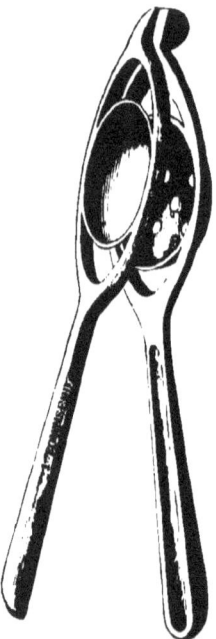

No. 3, Malleable Iron, Tinned...... ....$6 00 per dozen.

12 DOZEN IN A CASE.

IXL Lemon Squeezers.

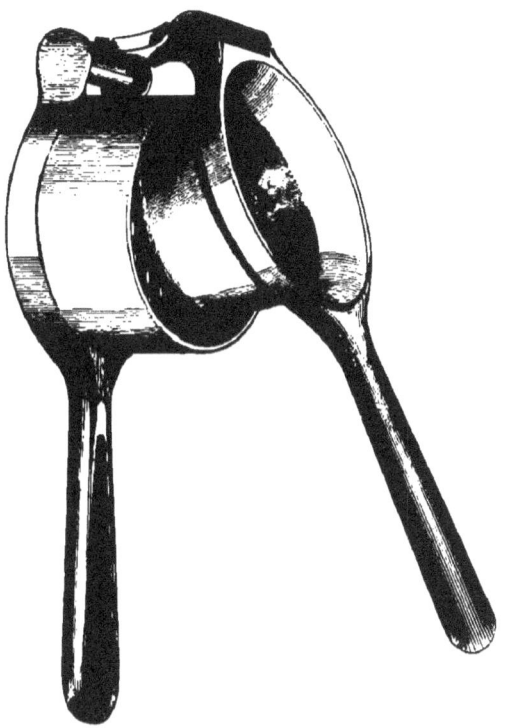

No. 1.

No. 1, Galvanized ....$3 50 per dozen.
" 2, " .... 5 00 "

12 DOZEN IN A CASE.

BOOT-JACKS.

No. 1.

No. 3.

	No. 1.	3
Japanned	$3 00	$1 30 per dozen.
Bronzed	3 75	"

FOOT RESTS.

| Japanned | $1 25 per dozen. |

DUMB-BELLS.

2 3 4 5 6 7 8 9 10 12 15 lbs. each.
18 20 25 30 40 50 " 8 cts per lb.

QUOITS.

	CAST IRON	MALLEABLE IRON.	MALLEABLE IRON GALVANIZED.
4½ inches	$0 60	$0 80	$1 20 per set
5 "	70	1 12	1 65 "
5½ "	85	1 44	2 16 "
6 "	1 10	1 75	2 56 "
6½ "	1 40	2 15	3 45 "
10 "		7 00	"

LATHE CARRIERS.

WITH STEEL SET SCREWS.

$0 40	$0 50	$0 60	$0 75	$0 90
¾	1	1¼	1½	1¾ inches.
$1 00	$1 15	$1 25	$1 35	
2	2¼	2½	2¾ inches.	
$1 50	$1 75	$2 00		
3	3½	4 inches		

WELL WHEELS.

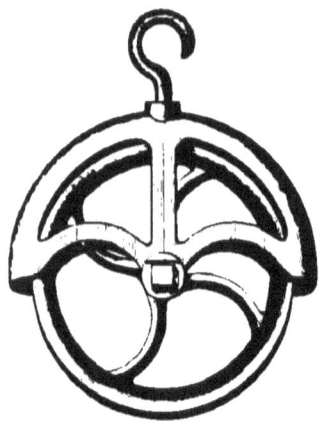

10 inches	$7 50 per dozen.
12 "	10 00 "

MELTING LADLES.

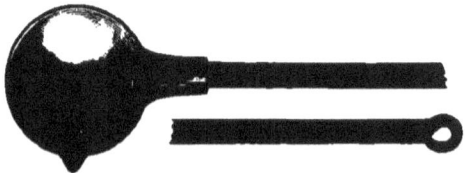

No. 1, 2½ inches	$2 00	per dozen.
" 2, 3 "	2 20	"
" 3, 3½ "	2 67	"
" 4, 4 "	3 20	"
" 5, 4½ "	3 85	"
" 6, 5 "	4 35	"
" 7, 6 "	6 40	"
" 8, 7 "	7 50	"

HAY-FORK PULLEYS.

SWIVEL EYE.

6 inches.. .... $5 00 per dozen.

5 DOZEN IN A BARREL.

OX BALLS.

SOLID.

No. 5.

No. 10.

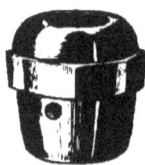

No. 15.

No. 20.

BRASS.

No. 5	$4 25	per gross.
" 10	5 37	"
" 15	7 87	"
" 20	10 75	"

MALLEABLE IRON, TINNED.

No. 5	$2 50	per gross.
" 10	3 50	"
" 15	4 50	"
" 20	6 00	"

UMBRELLA STANDS.

No. 7.

No. 8.

No. 3, Loose Dish.

No. 2.

	BRONZED.
No. 2	$4 25
" 3	4 00
" 7	2 50
" 8	3 00

DRUGGISTS' BRACKETS.

No. 3--6 inch Dish.
Green-and-Gold Bronzed .... $2 00 per pair.

No. 8, Swing--7 inch Dish.
Dark Bronzed .... $3 00 per pair.

No. 4, Swing -6½ inch Dish.
Green-and-Gold Bronzed .... $2 25 per pair.

No. 6, Swing--6½ inch Dish.
Dark Bronzed .... $3 00 per pair.

SHELF BRACKETS.

DARK BRONZED, WITH SCREWS.

No. 160.

No. 155, 3 by 4 inches	......	$1 75 per dozen pairs.
" 160, 4 " 5 "	......	2 25	"	"
" 165, 5 " 7 "	......	3 00	"	"
" 170, 6 " 7 "	......	3 75	"	"
" 175, 7 " 9 "	......	4 50	"	"
" 180, 8 " 10 "	......	5 50	"	"
" 185, 9 " 12 "	......	6 50	"	"

SHELF BRACKETS.

No. 55.

	JAPANNED.
No. 55, 4 by 5 inches	$1 50 per dozen pairs
" 65, 5 by 6 "	2 00 " "
" 75, 6 by 8 "	2 75 " "
" 85, 8 by 10 "	3 50 " "
" 95, 10 by 12 "	5 25 " "
" 105, 12 by 15 "	8 00 " "
" 115, 15 by 20 "	12 00 " "

SHELF BRACKETS.

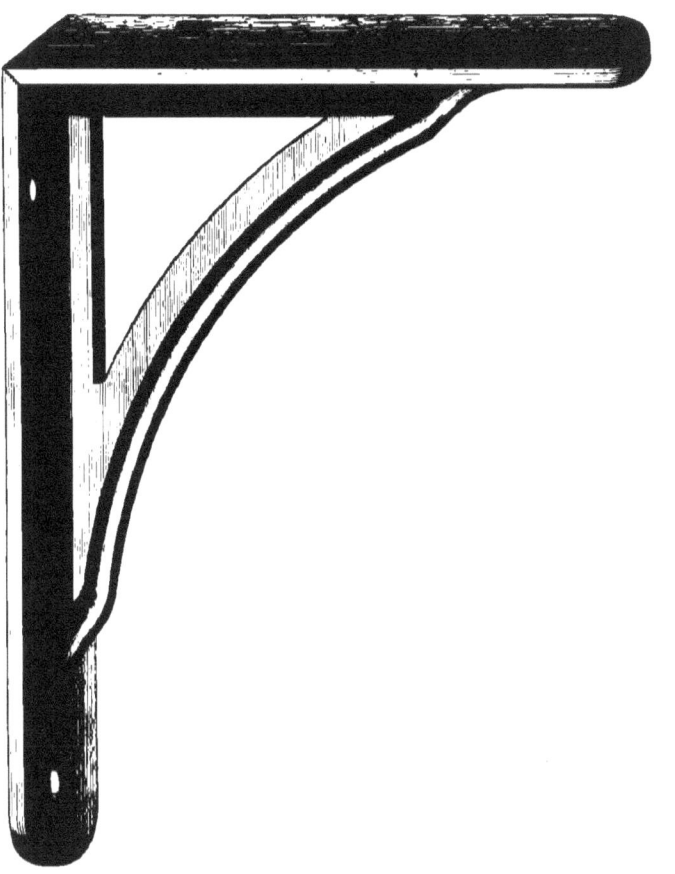

No. 60.

			JAPANNED.		
No. 40	3 by 4 inches		$1 00	per dozen pairs.	
" 60	5 by 6	"	2 16	"	"
" 80	6 by 8	"	3 00	"	"
" 100	8 by 10	"	4 80	"	"
" 120	8 by 12	"	5 40	"	"
" 135	10 by 12	"	8 00	"	"
" 150	12 by 15	"	10 00	"	"

SHELF BRACKETS.

No. 18.   *No. 5.*   *No. 27.*

No. 34.   *No. 26.*

	NOT JAPANNED.	JAPANNED.	BRONZED.	
No. 18, 4 by 6 inches.	......	$3 00	$3 50	per dozen pairs
" 5, 5 by 8 "	$3 72	4 20	5 00	" "
" 27, 6 by 8 "	5 00	6 00	7 00	" "
" 26, 7 by 10 "	6 00	7 00	8 00	" "
" 34, 5 by 8 "	6 00	7 00	8 00	" "
" 21, 9 by 12 "	8 40	10 00	11 00	" "

SHELF BRACKETS.

No. 23.

No. 17.

No. 32.

No. 8.

	NOT JAPANNED	JAPANNED	BRONZED
No. 23, 12¼ by 13½ inches	$12 00		
" 17, 10 by 13½ "	12 00	$14 00	$17 00 per dozen pairs
" 8, 13½ by 17 "	15 00	17 00	20 00
" 32.	6 00	7 80	10 80

BRACKETS.

No. 38.   *No. 37.*

	NOT JAPANNED.	JAPANNED.	BRONZED.	
No. 37, Size 7 by 10 inches	$7 00	$8 00	$9 50	per dozen pairs.
" 38, " " "	7 00	8 00	9 50	" "

No. 36.

FOR KEEPING IRON, STEEL, &c., SEPARATE.

No. 36, 12½ by 10 inches, not Japanned.................... $12 00 per dozen pairs.

MANTLE BRACKETS.

No. 14.

No. 35.

No. 11.

No. 15.

	NOT JAPANNED.	JAPANNED.	GOLD BRONZED.
No. 11, 5 by 8 inches.	$6 00	$7 50	$9 00 per dozen pairs.
" 15, 8 by 12 "	10 00	12 00	14 00 " "
" 14, 5½ by 8½ "	5 25	6 50	8 00 " "
" 35, 7 by 10 "	6 60	8 00	10 00 " "

PLEASE PASTE THIS OVER PAGE 162.

CARR, CRAWLEY & DEVLIN,
JUNE 3, 1878.

MALLEABLE IRON RINGS.

		JAPANNED.	TINNED.			JAPANNED	TINNED
1/2 inch,		$0 28	$0 35 per gro.	1 3/4 inches.	No. 0	$2 23	$2 68 per gro.
5/8 "		28	35	"	" 1	1 68	2 03 "
3/4 "		32	39	"	" 2	1 51	1 82 "
7/8 "	No. 8	37	46	"	" 3	1 28	1 55 "
"	" 7	42	52	"	" 4	1 10	1 32 "
"	" 8	44	54		" 5	1 03	1 24 "
1 "	" 7	50	60	2	" 0	2 40	2 88 "
1 1/8 "	" 8	54	64	"	" 1	1 88	2 27 "
"	" 7	60	70	"	" 2	1 71	2 05 "
1 1/4 "	" 3	1 00	1 20	"	" 3	1 44	1 74 "
"	" 4	88	1 07	2 1/4	" 4	1 23	1 48 "
"	" 5	77	94	"	" 1	3 00	4 32 "
"	" 6	68	81	2 1/2	" 0	2 67	3 33 "
"	" 7	57	69	"	" 1	3 67	4 83 "
"	" 8	56	68	3	" 0	3 00	3 67 "
"	" 2	1 33	1 60		" 1	4 67	5 67 "
1 1/2 "	" 3	1 13	1 36	3 1/2	" 0	4 00	4 83 "
"	" 4	1 02	1 23	"	" 1	5 33	6 50 "
"	" 5	85	1 03	4	" 0	4 33	5 50 "
"	" 6	78	94	"	" 1	6 00	9 00 "
"	" 7	64	78	4 1/2	" 0	5 00	7 50 "
				5	" 1	7 00	
				5 1/2	" 00	8 00)	5/8 inch.
					" 00	9 33 }	Wrought Iron.
					" 00	10 67)	

Roller Buckles.

FINE FINISH.

	3/8	1/2	5/8 inch.
No. 3, Tinned with German-Silver Roller			$1 50 per gross.
" 4, " " Tin Roller	$0 65	$0 85	1 10 "
" 5, Nickel Plated, with German-Silver Roller			2 00 "

SHOE BUCKLES,
WITHOUT ROLLER.

	¾	⅞	1 inch
Japanned	$0 58	$0 63	$0 69 per gross
Tinned	70	76	83 "

Skate Buckles,
WITH ROLLER.

			⅞ inch.
Japanned			$0 69 per gross
Tinned			82 "

Barrel Roller Buckles.

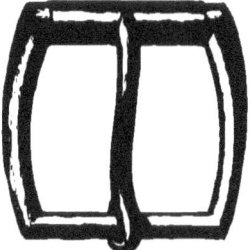

FINE FINISH.

	¾	⅞	1	1¼ inch.
No. 3, Japanned	$1 40	$1 50	$1 80	$2 45 per gross
" 4, " with Tinned Tongues,	1 73	2 00	2 40	3 20 "
" 5, Tinned	1 73	2 00	2 40	3 20 "
" 6, Japanned, with Tinned Tongues and German Silver Rollers	3 32	3 71	4 59	5 73
" 7, Tinned, with German Silver Rollers	3 30	3 69	4 59	5 93

Malleable Harness Buckles.

No 2.

	3/8	1/2	5/8	3/4	7/8	1	1¼	1½ inch.
Japanned...........	$0 38	$0 42	$0 51	$0 64	$0 77	$0 95	$1 47	$1 97 per gross.
Tinned, or Japanned with Tin'd Tongues	56	60	63	81	95	1 14	1 83	2 28 "

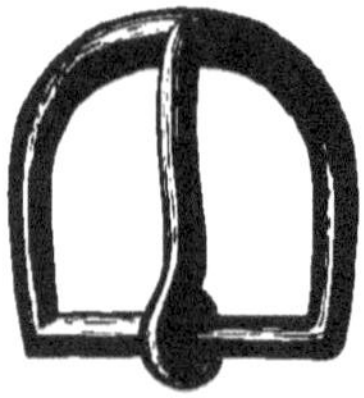

No. 3, Fine Finish.

	1/2	5/8	3/4	7/8	1	1¼ inch.
Japanned	$0 53	$0 55	$0 67	$0 83	$1 09	$1 67 per gross.
Tinned, or Japanned with Tin Tongues...................	80	84	96	1 13	1 40	2 07 "

Malleable Harness Buckles.

No. 3000, Extra Finish.

	½	⅝	¾	⅞	1	1¼
Japanned	$0 60	$0 63	$0 75	$0 92	$1 20	$1 90 per gross.
Tinned or Japanned, with Tin'd Tongues,	90	95	1 05	1 25	1 55	2 25 "

Malleable-Iron Roller Buckles.

N N.

	½	⅝	1	1⅛	1¼	1½	1¾	2 inch.
Japanned	$1 33	$1 40	$1 67	$1 97	$2 15	$2 43	$3 20	$3 73 per gross
Tinned	1 65	1 73	2 08	2 40	2 58	2 93	4 00	4 59 "

Malleable Roller Buckles.

No. 1.

	JAPANNED OR POLISHED.	TINNED.	
½ inch	$0 49	$0 64	per gross.
⅝ "	59	75	"
¾ "	63	79	"
⅞ "	79	93	"
1 "	95	1 15	"
1¼ "	1 17	1 56	"
1½ "	1 45	1 91	"
1¾ "	1 95	2 36	"
2 "	2 31	2 66	"
2¼ "	2 68	3 08	"
2½ "	2 97	3 39	"
2¾ "	3 30	3 76	"
3 "	3 59	4 09	"

No. 2.

	⅞	1	1¼	1½	
Japanned	$1 54	$1 72	$1 92	$2 23	per gross
Tinned	1 73	2 20	2 41	2 64	"

Malleable Barrel Roller Buckles.

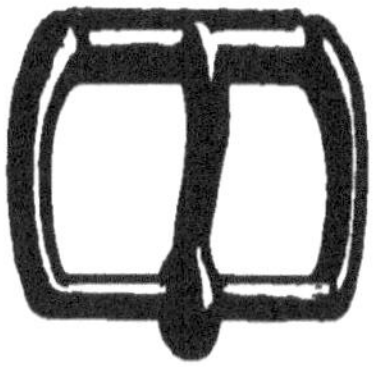

No. 1.

	½	⅝	¾	⅞	1	1⅛	1¼	1½	1¾	2 inches.	
Japanned	$0 49	$0 59	$0 68	$0 83	$0 97	$1 08	$1 27	$1 58	$2 12	$2 32	per gro.
Tinned or Japanned, with Tin'd Tongues, ...	0 64	0 75	0 84	0 97	1 15	1 32	1 58	2 05	2 36	2 67	"

No. 2.

	¾	⅞	1	1⅛ Inches.	
Japanned....................................	$0 95	$1 00	$1 18	$1 52	per gross.
Tinned...	1 17	1 22	1 33	1 70	"

SENSIBLE HARNESS BUCKLES.

Japanned	$0 75	$0 80	$1 00	$1 10	$1 40	$2 00	$3 00 per gro.
	½			1	1¼	1½ inch.
" with Tin'd Tongues.	1 00	1 20	1 49	1 84	2 40	3 36	4 40 "
Fine Tinned	1 01	1 08	1 33	1 52	1 92	2 87	4 12 "

SENSIBLE TRACE BUCKLES.

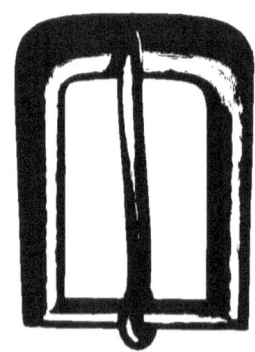

	1	1¼	1½	1¾ inch
Japanned	$0 18	$0 20	$0 25	$0 32	$0 43 per dozen.
Japanned with Tinned Tongues..	0 36	0 41	0 48	0 57	0 72 "
Fine Tinned	0 24	0 27	0 36	0 43	0 53 "

Sensible Combination-Loop Harness Buckles.

	⅝	¾	⅞	1	1¼	1½ inches.
Fine Tinned..... $1 17	$1 27	$1 77	$1 93	$2 42	$3 93	$5 13 per gross.

Sensible Combination-Loop Trace Buckles.

	⅞	1	1¼	1½	1¾ inches
Fine Tinned $0 37	$0 43	$0 55	$0 60	$0 71 per doz.

HORSE-SHOE TRACE BUCKLES.

No. 2.

	1	1¼	1½	1¾ inches.
Japanned $0 25	$0 27	$0 29	$0 36	$0 48 per dozen.
Tinned 39	43	52	62	78 "

Barrel Roller Trace Buckles.

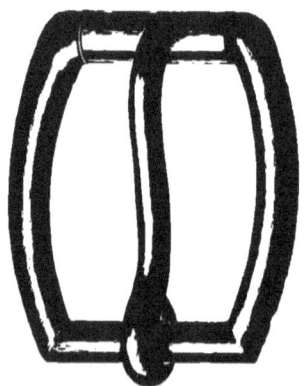

	1¼	1½	1¾	2 inches
Japanned	$0 48	$0 55	$0 69	$0 80 per dozen.
Tinned	65	71	87	1 00 "
Japanned, with Tinned Tongues	65	68	82	96 "

PHILADELPHIA TRACE BUCKLES.

	⅞	1	1¼	1¼	1½ inches.
Japanned	$0 18	$0 20	$0 25	$0 32	$0 43 per dozen.
Tinned	24	27	36	43	53 "

MULE PORT BITS.

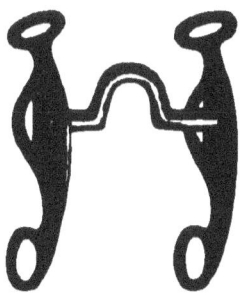

No. 641.

Japanned .... $1 20 per dozen.
Tinned .... 1 47 "

RING BITS.

	POLISHED.	JAPANNED.	TINNED.
No. 1, 3 lb., 1½ inch., Loose Ring	$0 53	$0 53	$0 67 per dozen.
" 5, 5½ lb., 2 inch , "		71	93 "
" 6, 6½ lb., 2 inch , "		90	1 07 "
" 25, 8½ inch, 2½ inch, Fast Ring		1 20	1 40 "
" 8, 6½ lb., 2½ inch , Loose Ring, Stiff Mouth		90	1 07 "
" 9, 7½ lb., 2½ inch , "		1 07	1 20 "
" 11, 4½ lb., 4½ inch , " Twist'd Mouth		68	90 "
" 50, 2½ inch		1 07	1 20 "

SNAFFLE BITS.

	JAPANNED	TINNED.
No. 15, 7, lbs	$1 07	$1 50 per dozen.
" 16, 7, lbs, Butted		1 60 "

PORT BITS.

No. 100, Fine Tinned .... $1 73 per dozen.

No. 105, Fine Tinned .... $1 73 per dozen.

PORT BITS.

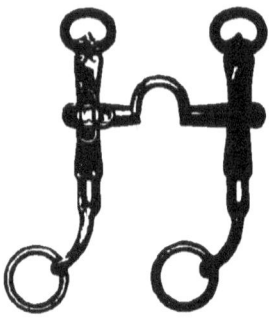

No. 110, Fine Tinned..$1 73 per dozen.

No. 115, Fine Tinned..$1 73 per dozen.

PORT BITS.

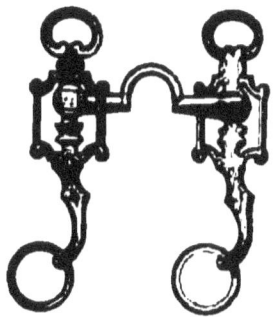

No. 120, Fine Tinned.. $1 47 per dozen.

No. 125, Fine Tinned........................ $1 47 per dozen.

REIN SWIVELS.

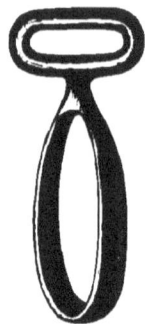

Nos. 9, 19 and 29.   *Nos. 15, 25 and 35.*

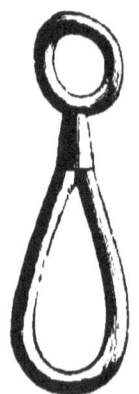

Nos. 30, 40 & 50.   *Nos. 0, 10 & 20.*   *Nos. 1000, 1010 & 1020.*

	No. 0	9	15	30	1000
Iron Japanned	$0 90	$1 07	$0 90	$0 90	$0 90 per gross.
	No. 10	19	25	40	1010
Malleable Iron Japanned	1 10	1 07	1 33	1 10	1 10
	No. 20	29	35	50	1020
Tinned	1 72	2 13	1 72	1 72	1 72

BOLT HOOKS.

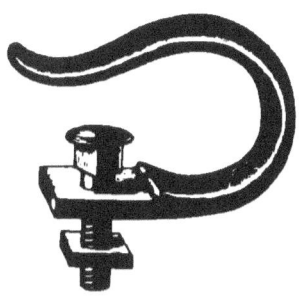 

Nos. 40, 50 and 150.   *Nos. 45, 55 and 155.*

No. 40, Grey Iron, Japanned .... $0 45 per dozen.
" 45, " " " .... 50 "
" 50, Malleable Iron, Japanned .... 60 "
" 55, " " " .... 73 "
" 150, " " Fine Tinned .... 66 "
" 155, " " " .... 80 "

TERRETS.

 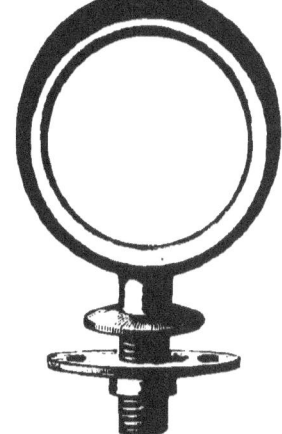

Nos. 40, 50 and 150.   *Nos. 45, 55 and 155.*

No. 40, Grey Iron, Japanned .... $0 35 per dozen.
" 45, " " " .... 40 "
" 50, Malleable Iron, Japanned .... 49 "
" 55, " " " .... 66 "
" 150, " " Fine Tinned .... 53 "
" 155, " " " .... 72 "

Triangular Cock-Eyes,
WITH ROLLERS.

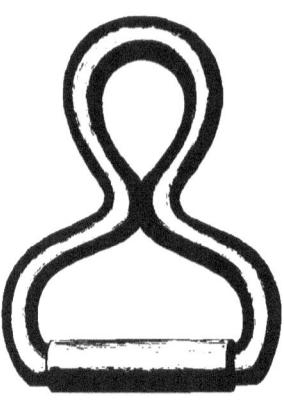

	1½	1¾ inches.
Japanned	$0 27	$0 32 per dozen.
Tinned	36	41 "

Cock-Eyes with Screws.

	1¼	1½	1¾	2 inches.
Japanned	$0 30	$0 32	$0 36	$0 49 per dozen.
Tinned	39	40	44	60 "

HAME FASTENERS.

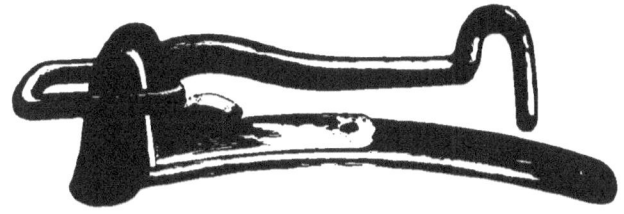

No. 1 ..... $1 85 per dozen.
" 2 .... 2 00 "

BREECHING LOOPS.

	JAPANNED	TINNED
1¼ inches, 5-16ths thick....	$0 50	$0 70 per dozen.
1½ " 3-8ths "	65	85 "
2 " 3-8ths "	80	1 05 "

HALTER BOLTS.

JAPANNED.

⅞	1	1¼	1½ inches.
$0 30	$0 43	$0 56	$0 67 per gross.

TRACE LOOPS.

	JAPANNED.	TINNED.
1 inch	$0 35	$0 55 per dozen.
1¼ "	43	68 "
1½ "	54	75 "

HALTER AND TRACE SQUARES.

	JAPANNED	TINNED
⅝ by 1 inch	$0 90	$1 20 per gross
1 by 1 "	1 15	1 60 "
1 by 1 " No. 1	1 60	2 00 "
1 by 1 " 2, Heavy	1 80	2 20 "
1 by 1½ "	2 00	2 55 "
1 by 2 "	4 00	5 50 "

MALLEABLE D's.

	JAPANNED	TINNED	
⅝ inch	$0 48	$0 70	per gross.
¾ "	55	80	"
⅞ "	66	93	"
1 "	87	1 20	"
1¼ "	1 33	1 73	"
1½ "	1 73	2 27	"
1¾ "	2 07	2 67	"
2 "	2 50	3 25	"
2½ "	3 00	4 00	"

HALTER TRIANGLES.

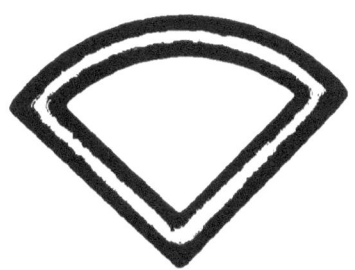

1 inch, Japanned .... $2 00 per gross   1½ inch, Japanned .... $2 75 per gross

STIRRUPS.

	JAPANNED	TINNED	
No. 30	$2 00		per dozen.
" 40	1 20		"
" 51	1 50		"
" 63	1 75		"
" 70	1 75	$3 00	"
" 72	1 50		"
" 62, Hobby-Horse	63		

CARRIAGE HINGES.

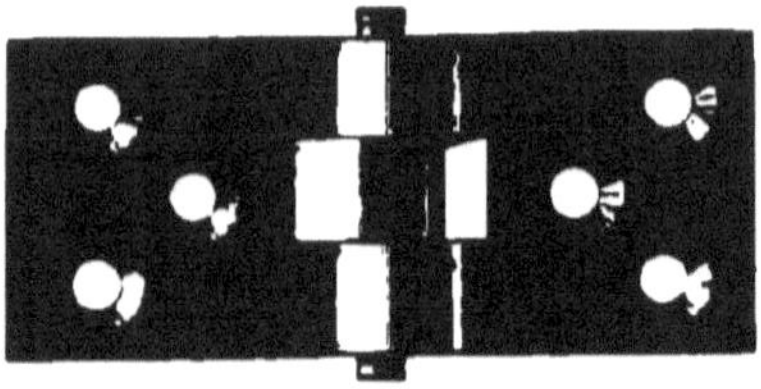

No. 1.

1¼ inch, 1 inch wide	$0 90	per dozen.
1½ " 1 "	95	"
1¾ " 1⅛	1 00	"
2 " 1⅛	1 15	"
2¼ " 1¼	1 30	"
2½ " 1¼	1 50	"
2¾ " 1¼	1 65	"
3 1¼	1 85	"

No. 2.

1¾ inch, 1¼ inch wide	$1 20	"
2 " 1¼ "	1 35	"
2¼ " 1¼ "	1 55	"

No. 3.

DOUBLE JOINTED—RIGHT AND LEFT.

2 inch, 1½ inch wide	$2 00	per dozen.
2½ " 1½ "	2 37	"
3 " 1½	2 75	"

COACH HINGES.

WITHOUT HOLES

2¼ inch, 1½ inch wide	$2 50	per dozen.
2½ " 1½ "	3 00	"
3 " 1½ "	3 25	"
3½ " 1½ "	3 50	"
4 " 1½ "	4 25	"
5 " 1½ "	5 00	"

Carriage-Door Dove-Tails.

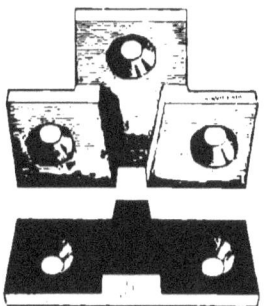

No. 1.

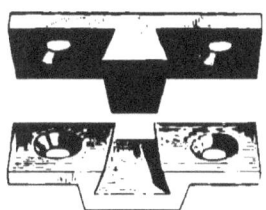

No. 3.

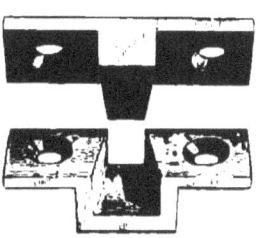

No. 4.

No. 1 .... $1 00 per dozen.
 " 3   85   "
 " 4   85   "

LAZY BACK IRONS.

Nos. 1 and 2.

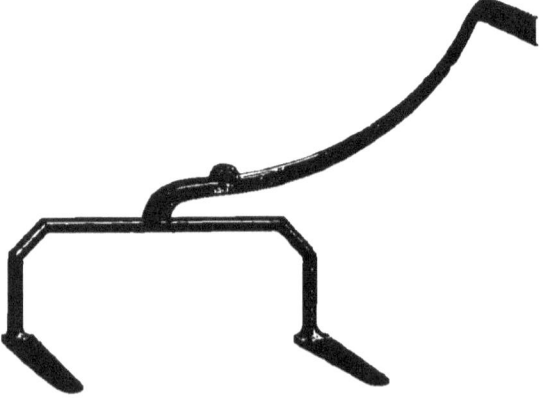

No. 3.

No 1, ¼ inch	$9 00	per dozen pairs.
" 2, ⅜ "	10 50	" "
" 3, ½ "	13 50	" "

JUMP SEAT IRONS.

GREGG & BOWE'S PATENT.

FRONT. BACK.

No. 1—$5 75 per set.

SCHAEFFER'S PATENT.

FRONT. BACK.

No. 2—$5 25 per set.

YOKE TIPS.

	FINE TINNED.	JAPANNED.
¾ inch	$2 50	$1 50 per dozen pairs
1 "	2 88	1 88 " "
1¼ "	3 25	2 25 " "

SWINGLETREE TIPS.

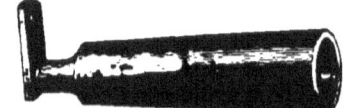

No. 1.

No. 2.

No. 3.

	FINE TINNED.	JAPANNED.
⅞ inch	$2 80	$1 80 per dozen pairs
⅞ "	3 00	2 00 " "
1 "	3 35	2 35 " "

SHAFT TIPS.

	FINE TINNED.	JAPANNED.
⅞ inch	$2 00	$1 25 per dozen pairs.
1 "	2 25	1 50 " "

POLE TIPS.

	FINE TINNED.	JAPANNED.
1 inch	$4 00	$2 35 per dozen.
1⅛ "	4 25	2 75 "
1¼ "	4 50	3 15 "
1⅜ "	5 00	3 50 "
1½ "	5 50	3 75 "

SCREW CLAMPS.

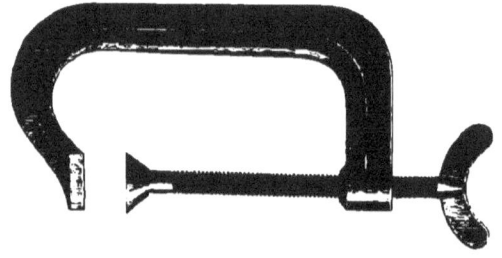

No.		Opens				
No 1.	Opens	2¼ inches		$3 50	per dozen.
" 2.	"	3¼ "		5 00	"
" 2½.	"	4¼ "		5 50	"
" 3.	"	4¼ "		6 00	"
" 3½.	"	5 "		7 00	"
" 4.	"	6 "		8 00	"
" 5.	"	7 "		9 50	"
" 6.	"	8½ "		12 50	"
" 7.	"	10½ "		14 00	"
" 8.	"	12½ "		15 50	"

TOP PROPS.

Nos. 26 and 36.

No. 26, with No. 4 Nuts and No. 4 Rivets .... $0 50 per set.
" 36, " 5 " " 5 " .... 40 "

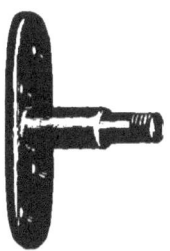 

Nos. 21 and 31.

No. 21, with No. 4 Nuts and No. 4 Rivets.. $0 45 per set.
" 31, " 5 " " 5 " .... 35 "

TOP PROPS.

 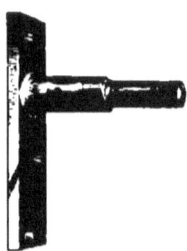

Nos. 22 and 32.

No. 22, with No. 4 Nuts and No. 4 Rivets.. $0 50 per set.
" 32, "   " 5 "   " 5 "   40   "

Nos. 25 and 35.

No. 25, with No. 4 Nuts and No. 4 Rivets.. $0 50 per set.
" 35, "   " 5 "   " 5 "   40   "

TOP PROPS.

 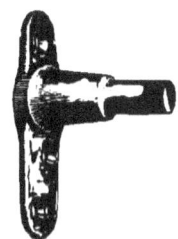

Nos. 27 and 37.

No. 27, with No. 4 Nuts and No. 4 Rivets .... $0 50 per set.
" 37, "   " 5   "   " 5 " .... 40 "

TOP-PROP NUTS.

No. 4, Fine Tinned .... $4 50 per gross.
" 5, " Japanned   3 50   "

TOP-PROP RIVETS.

No. 4, Fine Tinned .... $3 50 per gross
" 5, " Japanned .... 2 00   "

APRON HOOKS AND RINGS.

	JAPANNED.	TINNED.
Malleable Iron	$1 20	$1 50 per gross.

Chase's Patent Hollow Wrench,
FOR CONTAINING OIL.

GALVANIZED

1, 1¼, 1½ inch. $6 00 per dozen.

IRON CARRIAGE BANDS.

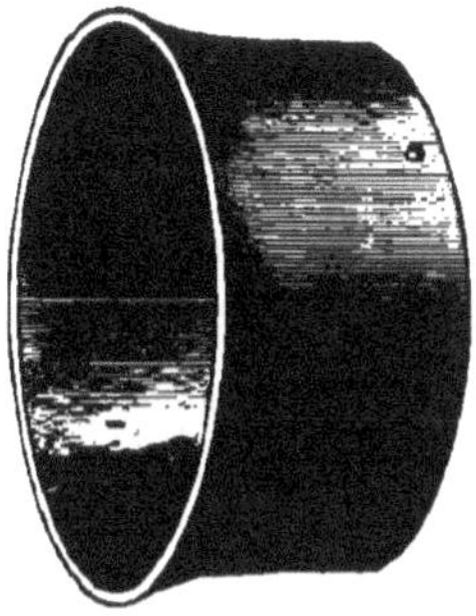

Bell, 1¾ wide.

	TURNED.	FINE TINNED.
1¾ inch	$0 52	$0 77 per set.
1⅞ "	52	77 "
2 "	52	77 "
2⅛ "	52	77 "
2¼ "	52	77 "
2⅜ "	52	77 "
2½ "	52	77 "
2⅝ "	52	77 "
2¾ "	52	77 "
2⅞ "	52	77 "
3 "	52	77 "
3⅛ "	57	82 "
3¼ "	62	87 "

IRON CARRIAGE BANDS.

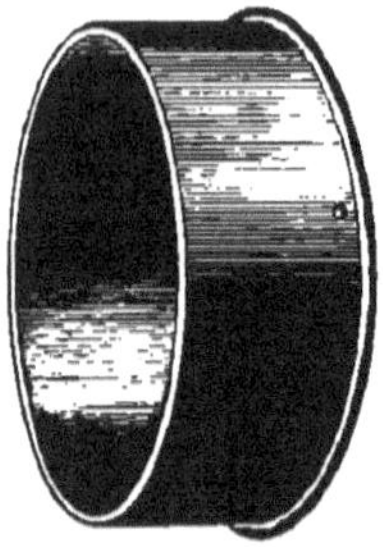

No. 5, 1½ inches wide.

	TURNED.	FINE TINNED.
2⅛ inch	$0 40	$0 65 per set.
2¼ "	40	65 "
2⅜ "	40	65 "
2½ "	40	65 "
2⅝ "	40	65 "
2¾ "	40	65 "
2⅞ "	40	65 "
3 "	40	65 "
3⅛ "	45	70 "
3¼ "	50	75 "
3⅜ "	55	80 "
3½ "	60	85 "

IRON CARRIAGE BANDS.

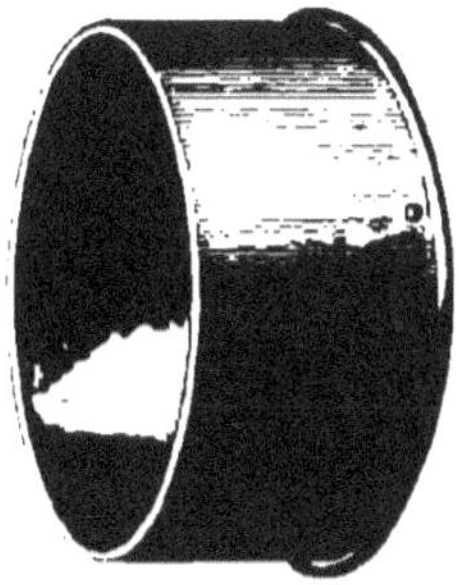

No. 6, 1⅜ inches wide.

	TURNED.	FINE TINNED.
2 inch	$0 45	$0 70 per set.
2⅛ "	45	70 "
2¼ "	45	70
2⅜ "	45	70
2½ "	45	70
2⅝ "	45	70
2¾ "	45	70
2⅞ "	45	70
3 "	45	70
3⅛ "	50	75
3¼ "	55	80
3⅜ "	60	85
3½ "	65	90
3⅝ "	70	75
3¾ "	75	1 00
3⅞ "	80	1 65
4 "	85	1 15

IRON CARRIAGE BANDS.

TURNED.

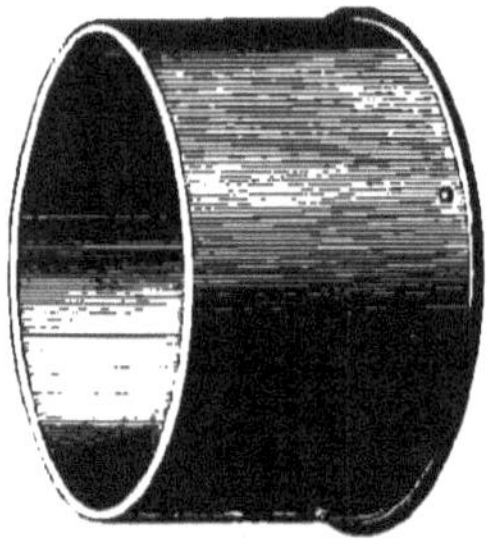

Nos. 7 and 8.

	No. 7. 2 Inches Wide.	No. 8. 2¼ Inches Wide.	
2¼ inch	$0 50	$	per set.
2⅜ "	50		"
2½ "	50	60	"
2⅝ "	50	60	"
2¾ "	50	60	"
2⅞ "	50	60	"
3 "	50	60	"
3¼ "	55	65	"
3⅜ "	60	70	"
3½ "	65	75	"
3⅝ "	70	80	"
3¾ "	80	90	"
4 "	90	1 00	"
4¼ "	1 05	1 15	"
4½ "	1 25		"
4¾ "	1 45		"
5 "	1 65		"

IRON CARRIAGE BANDS.

TURNED.

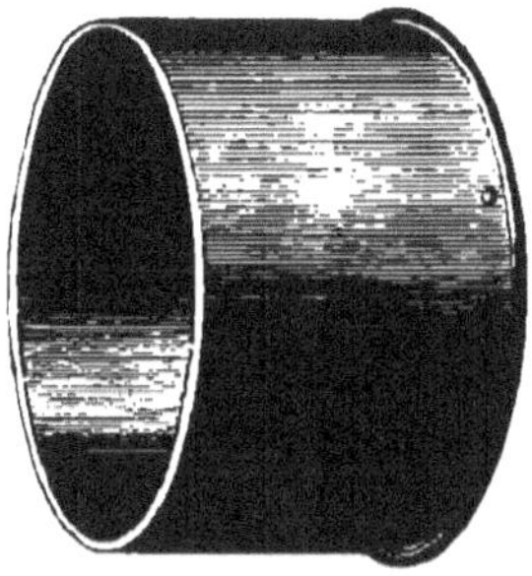

No. 9, 2½ inches wide.

2¼ inch	$0 75	per set.
2½ "	75	"
2¾ "	75	"
3 "	75	"
3⅛ "	80	"
3¼ "	85	"
3⅜ "	90	"
3½ "	95	"
3¾ "	1 05	"
4 "	1 15	"
4¼ "	1 25	"
4½ "	1 35	"

IRON CARRIAGE BANDS.

TURNED.

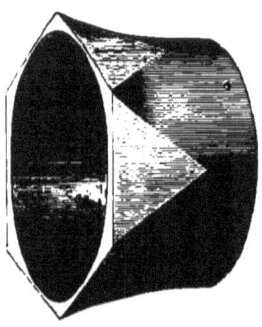

Nos. 7½ and 8½.
Nos. 7¾ and 8¾, Jagged.

2 ROUND AND 2 HEXAGON IN A SET.

	No. 7½. 2 Inches Wide.	No. 8½. 2½ Inches Wide.	No. 7¾. 2 Inches Wide.	No. 8¾. 2½ Inches Wide.
2¼ inch	$0 75	$	$1 00	$ per set.
2⅜ "	75	80	1 00	1 05 "
2½ "	75	80	1 00	1 05 "
2⅝ "	75	80	1 00	1 05 "
3 "	75	80	1 00	1 05 "
3¼ "		85		1 10 "
3⅜ "		90		1 15 "
3½ "		1 00		1 25 "
3⅝ "		1 10		1 35 "
4 "		1 20		1 45 "
4¼ "		1 30		1 55 "

IRON CARRIAGE BANDS.

TURNED AND JAGGED.

No. 9½, 2½ inches wide.

2 ROUND AND 2 HEXAGON IN A SET.

2¼ inch	$1 15	per set
2½ "	1 15	"
2¾ "	1 15	"
3 "	1 15	"
3⅛ "	1 20	"
3¼ "	1 25	"
3⅜ "	1 30	"
3½ "	1 35	"
3⅝ "	1 45	"
3¾ "	1 50	"
4 "	1 55	"
4¼ "	1 65	"
4½ "	1 75	"

CARRIAGE WRENCHES.

No. 2.

¾,   ⅞,   ⅞,   1,   1⅛,   1¼ inches.

No. 3.

⅞,   2,   1⅛,   1¼ inches.

No. 1.

1⅛,   1¼,   1⅞,   2,   2⅛,   2¼ inches.

Thimble Skein Wrenches.
GREY IRON.

No. 4.

2⅛,   2⅛,   2⅜,   2¼ inches

MACHINERY WRENCHES.

Nos. 4,   5,   6,   7,   8,
1¼ by 1¼,   ⅞ by 1,   1 by ⅞,   ⅞ by ⅞,   ⅞ by ¾ inch.

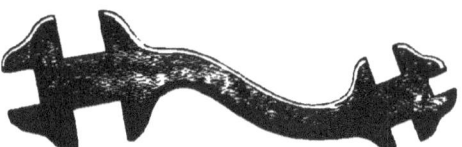

Nos. 21 and 22.

No. 21 .... For Nuts ⅜ to 1¼ inch.
" 22 .... " ⅜ to 1¼ inch.

Nos. 9,   10,   11,   12,   13,   14,
¾ by ¾   ⅞ by ⅞,   ⅞ by 1,   1¼ by 1¼,   1¼ by 1¼,   1¼ by 1¼ inch.

SWINGLETREE PLATES.

SINGLE

IN 10 LB. BOXES.

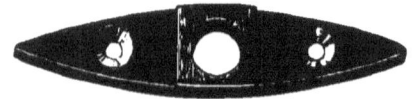

No. 1.

Nos. 2 and 3.
⅞, ⅞ inch Hole.

No. 4.

SWINGLETREE PLATES.
DOUBLE.
IN 10 LB. BOXES.

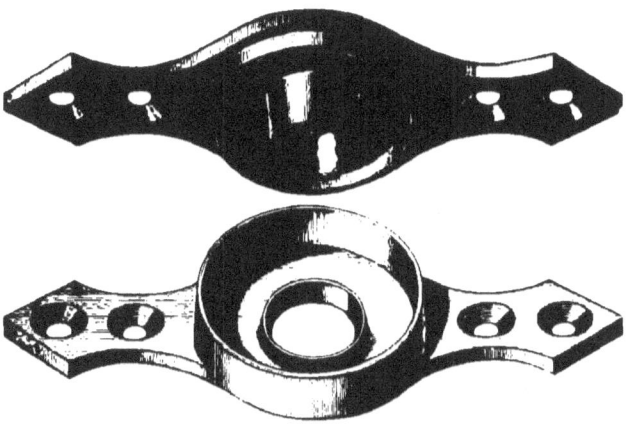

No. 2.

No. 1, Shallow Pattern .... 1¼, 1½, 1¾, 2¼ inch.
" 2, Deep   "   ....1½, 1¾, 1¾, 2¼, 2½, 3 "

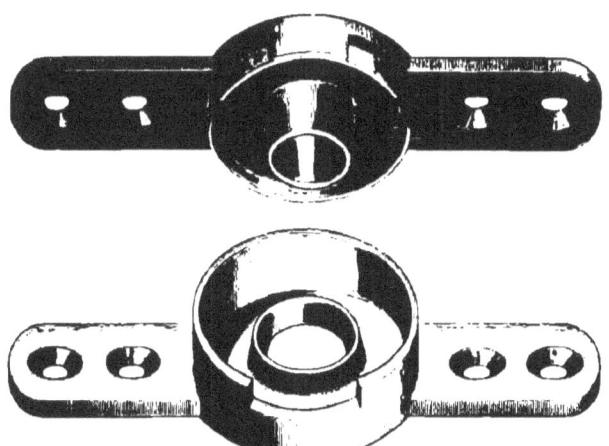

No. 3, 1½ inches.

AXLE CLIP BARS.

IN 10 LB. BOXES.

No. 2.

¾, 1, 1¼, 1½, 1¾ inches.

No. 5.

¾, 1, 1¼, 1½ inches.

No. 7.

1, 1¼, 1½, 1¾, 1¾ inches.

AXLE CLIP BARS.

IN 10 LB. BOXES.

No 4.

⅞,   1,   1¼,   1½,   1¾,   1⅞ inches.

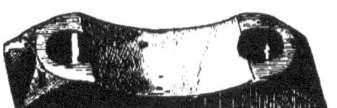

No. 3.

⅞,   1,   1¼,   1½ inches.

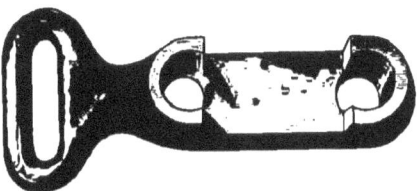

No. 6.

¾,   1,   1¼,   1½ inches.

COCK EYES.

IN 10 LB. BOXES.

No. 1.

No. 2.

No. 3.

COCK EYES.
IN 10 LB. BOXES.

No. 7.

No. 9.

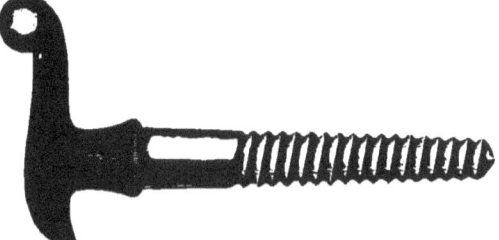

No. 8.

SWINGLETREE HOOKS.

No. 1. ⅔ Size.

COCK EYES.

IN 10 LB. BOXES.

No. 4

No. 5

No. 6

BOLSTER PLATES.

CAST IRON

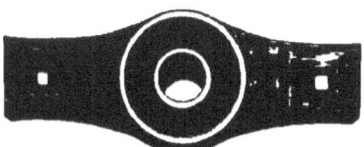

(HALF.)

No. 56, 9¼ inches Long, 3¼ inches Circle .... $0 06 per lb.
" 57, 13½ " 3½ " .... 06 "
" 50, 13½ " 4½ " 06 "

MALLEABLE IRON.

No. 1, 18 inches Long, for 1¼ inch Axle
" 2, 21 " " 2¼ "

SWINGLETREE PLATES.

No. 5, 1½ inch.

STEP PLATES.

No. 5.
3¼ by 5 inches.

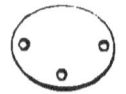

No. 3.
3¼ by 4½ inches.

No. 6.
3¾ inches.

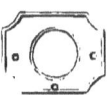

No. 1.
3¼ by 4¼ inches.

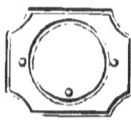

No. 2.
4¼ by 5¼ inches.

No. 4.
4¼ by 5¼.

No. 25.
3 by 4 inches

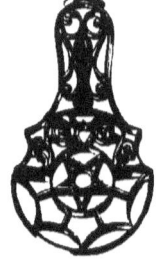

Nos. 9, 10, 11.
No. 9, 6½ by 11¼ inches.
No. 10, 9 by 15½ "
No. 11, 9 by 9 inches, without Toe Piece.

STEP PLATES.

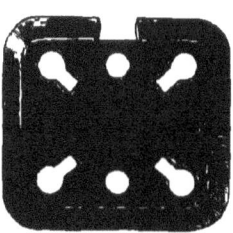

Nos. 15 and 16.
3 by 3½. 4 by 4¼ inches.

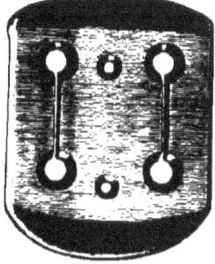

Nos. 7 and 8.
3 by 4. 3½ by 4¼ inches.

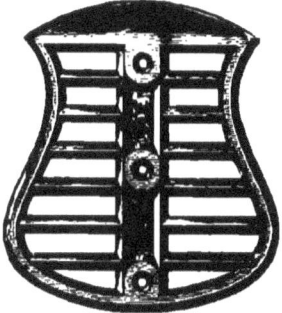

No. 14.
4 by 4¼ inches.

No. 12.
4½ by 5 inches.

No. 18.
4 by 8½ inches.

No. 19.
3½ by 8 inches.

CARRIAGE STEPS.

No. 387.

No. 377--2½ inch Lip.
No. 377½--2 inch Lip.

CARRIAGE STEPS

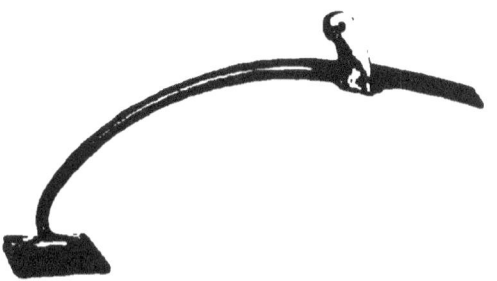

No. 20.

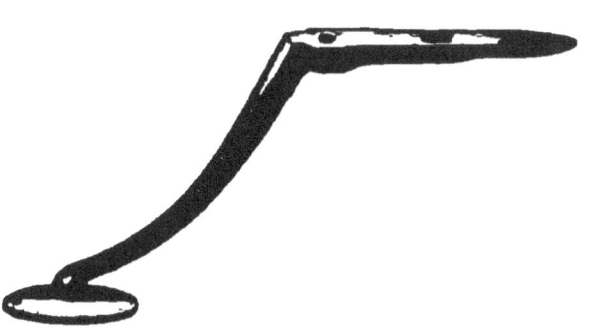

No. 21.

CARRIAGE STEPS.

No. 378.

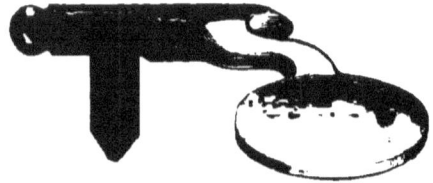

No. 19.

SLEIGH STEPS.

No. 17.
5¼ by 10¼ inches.

RUB IRONS.

No 2—5¼ inches.

No. 5, 6 inches.

No. 19, 7 inches.

No. 20, 6 inches.

No. 4, 6¼ inches.

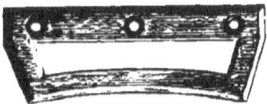

No. 10—6 inches.

No. 11, 5¼ inches.

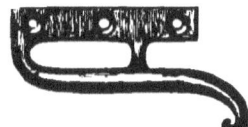

No. 17, 5½ inches.

No. 14, 5½ inches.

No. 21, 7 inches.

SWINGLETREE CLEVICES.

Nos. 5 and 6.

No. 3, 1 in., 4½ in. long, with Round Pin.   No. 5, 1½ in., 4½ in. long, with Self-Fastening Pin.
"   4, 2 in., 5   "   "   "   "   "   6, 2 in., 5   "   "   "   "   "

STAKE IRONS.

1 inch has 2 Square Holes.
1 inch has 4 Countersunk Holes.
2 inch has 4 Square Holes.

STAKE RINGS.   SEAT HOOKS.

1½ by 1½ inch.   1 by 1½ inch.
                         3½ and 4 inches long.

SIDEBOARD STAPLES.

1½ inch.

BOW STAPLES.

1¼ and 1½ inch.

BODY ROD PLATES.

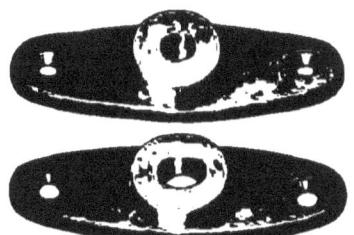

SPRING CLIP PLATES.

No 1.
1¼, 1⅜, 1½ inches.

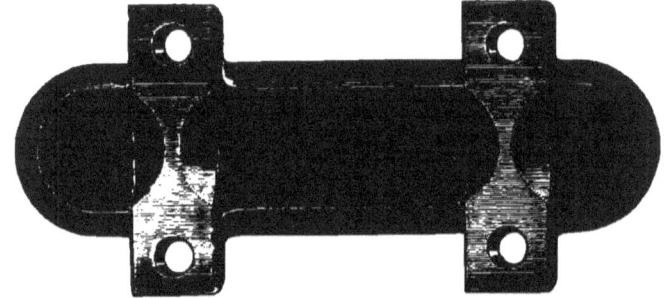

No. 2.
1¼, 1½ inches.

No. 3.
1¼, 1¾, 2 inches.

SPRING CLIP BARS.

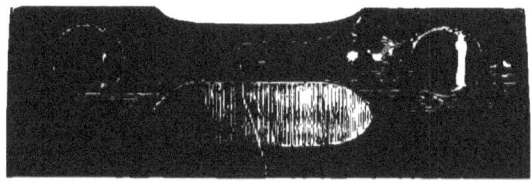

1¼, 2, 2¼, 2½, 3 inches

SPRING BLOCKS.

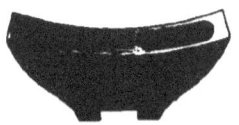

For 1¼, 2, 2¼, 2½, inch Springs.

SPRING SHACKLES.

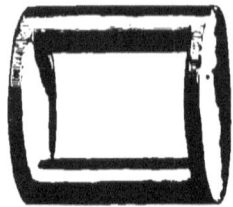

1¼, 1⅜, 1½, 1¾ inches

SPRING SHACKLE HOLDERS.

No. 1—1¼, 1⅜, 1½, 1¾ inches.   No. 2—1¼ inch, for 1 inch Wood.
" 3—1½ " 1¼ "
" 4—1⅝ " 1 "
" 5—1⅝ " 1¼ "

SEAT RAIL PLATES.

SHAFT SHACKLES.

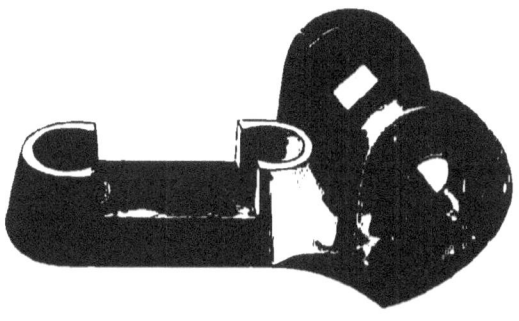

No. 1—For 1 inch Shaft, 1¼ inch Axle.
" 2— For 1¼   "   1½ "

Umbrella-Holder and Socket.

PERCH PLATES,
IN 10-LB. BOXES.

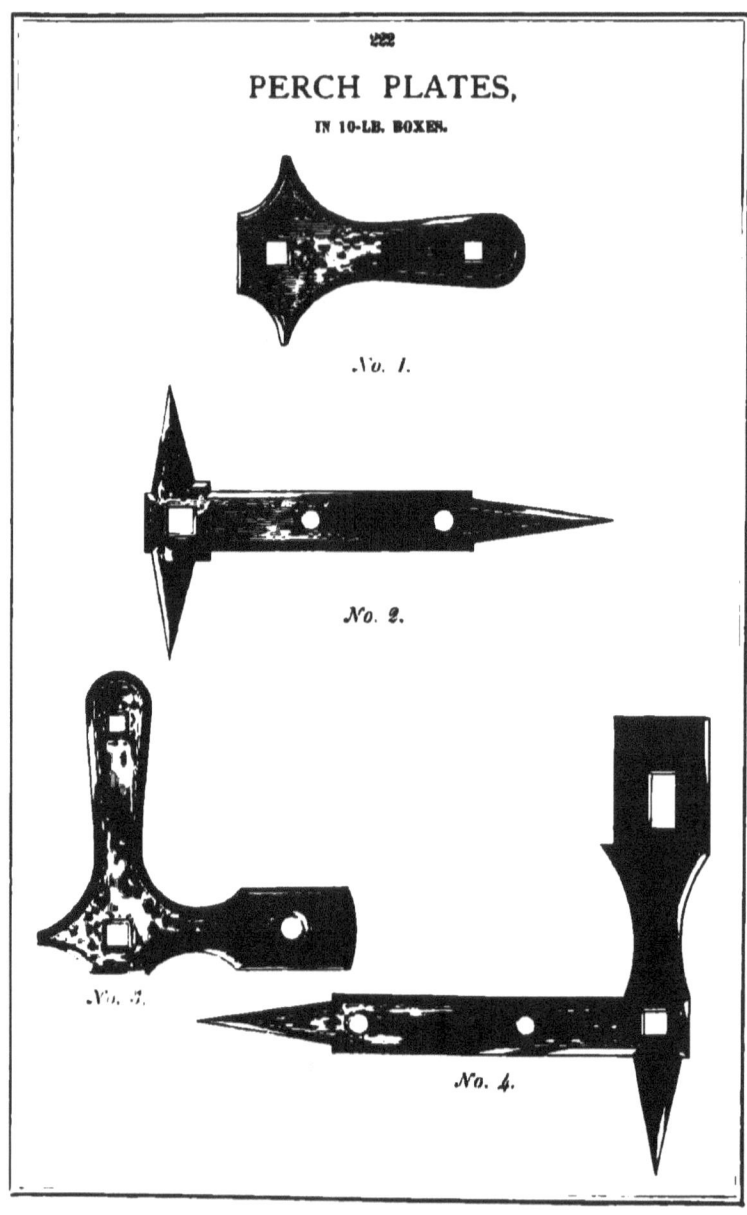

No. 1.

No. 2.

No. 3.

No. 4.

FELLOE PLATES.

MALLEABLE IRON.

IN 10-LB. BOXES.

Nos. 8,   7,   6,   0
    ⅝,   ⅞,   1¼, 1½ inches

WROUGHT IRON.

IN 10 LB. BOXES.

⅝,   ¾,   1¼,   1½,   1,   1¾,   1,   1½   2 inches
                                Steel

FOOTMAN LOOPS.

IN 10-LB. BOXES.

No. 1, Light   ⅞,   1,   1½   1½ inches
" 2, Heavy   1¼, 1½   2"
                1½ inch Double

HOLDBACKS.

IN 10-LB. BOXES.

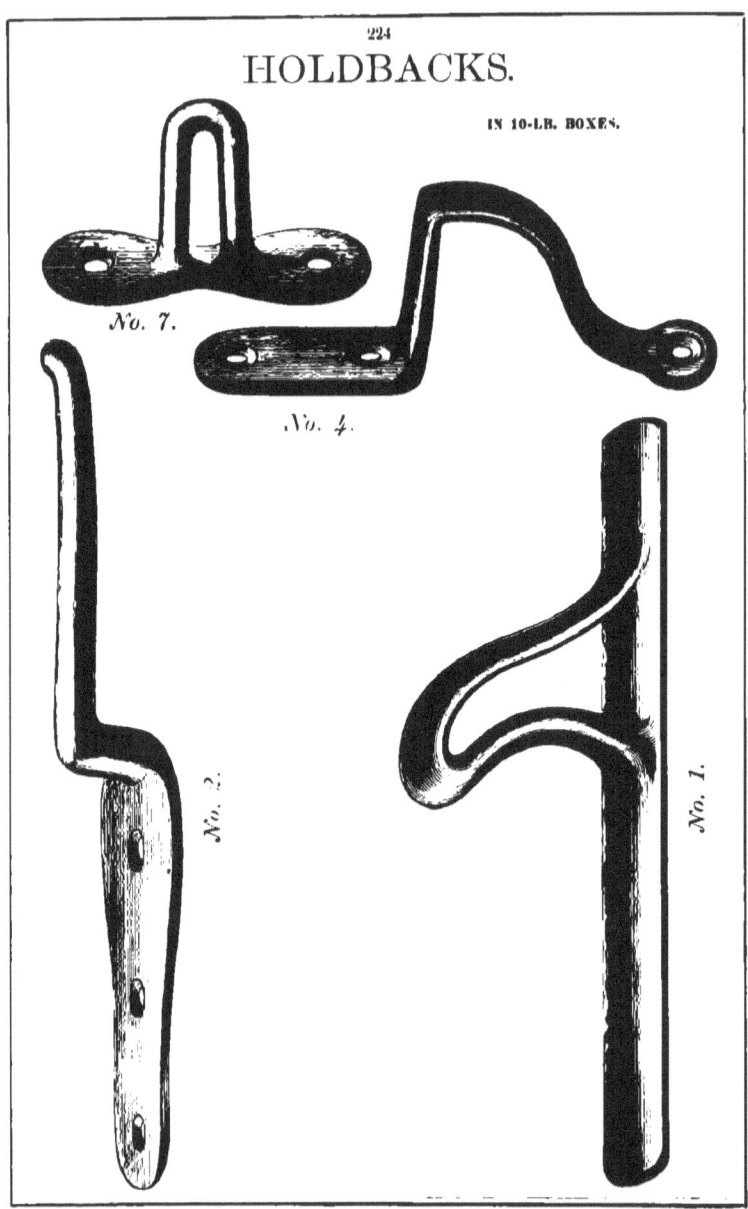

HOLDBACKS.
IN 10-LB. BOXES.

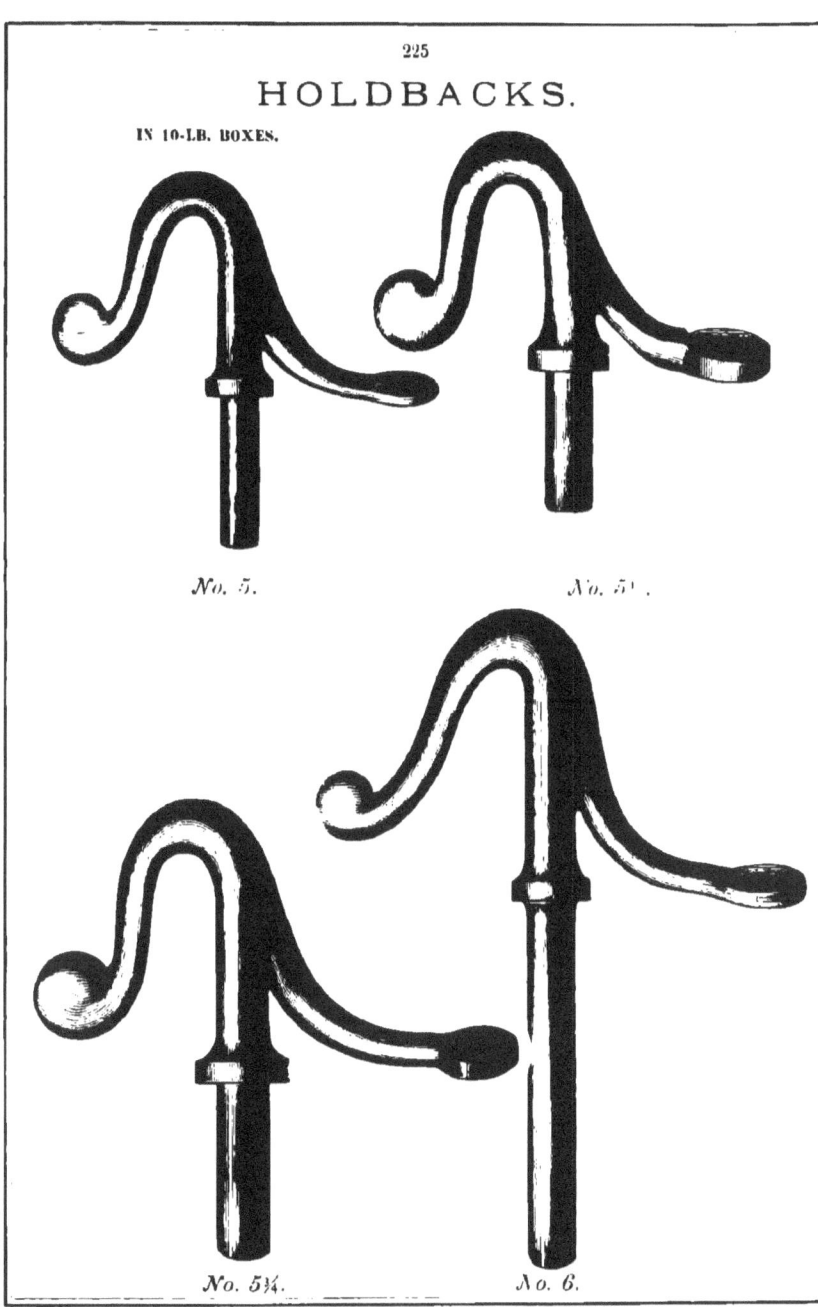

No. 5.   No. 5¼.

No. 5½.   No. 6.

ROUND FERRULES.

IN 10-LB. BOXES.

5/8, 3/4, 7/8, 1, 1 1/8, 1 1/4, 1 3/8, 1 1/2, 1 5/8, 1 3/4 inch Inside at Large End.
3/4, 7/8, 1, 1 1/8, 1 1/4 inch, Closed End, " "

SQUARE FERRULES.

IN 10-LB BOXES.

1, 1 1/4 inch.

OBLONG FERRULES.

IN 10-LB. BOXES.

3/4 by 1, 1 by 1 1/4, 1 1/16 by 1 3/8 inches.
1 1/16 by 2 1/8, 1 3/8 by 2 3/8, 1 5/8 by 2 1/4 "

HOOK FERRULES.

1 1/8, 1 1/4 inch.

SWINGLERREE FERRULES

WITH EYES.

1 1/4, 1 3/8, 1 1/2, inches.

SAND BANDS.

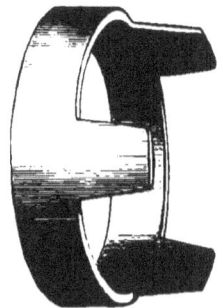

No. 1.

2,   2¼,   2½,   2¾,   3,   3¼,   3½,   4,   4½ inches.

No. 2.

2,   2¼,   2½,   2¾,   3 inches.

AXLE PLATES.

12, 14, 16 inches.

AXLE NUTS.

For ¾, 1, 1¼, 1¼, 1¼, 1¼, 1⅝, 1¾, 2, 2¼, 2½, 3 inch Axles.

Tailboard Staples.   Collars.

1½, 2½ inches.   1½, 1¼, 1¾, 2, 2¼, 2½, 2¾, 3 inches.

BEVEL CORNER PLATES.

T PLATES.
IN 10-LB. BOXES

2½ by 4½ inches   4½ by 5 inches   5 by 6 inches

CORNER PLATES.
IN 10-LB. BOXES.

16.   2½.   2½   5½.   6 inches

KNEE PLATES.
IN 10-LB. BOXES.

2½.   3   4½   6 inches

Finishing 9 inch 2 cents each

SINGLE CHECK LOOPS.

IN 10-LB. BOXES.

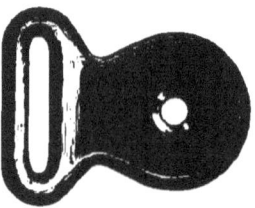

⅝, ⅞, 1, 1¼, 1½ inches.

DOUBLE CHECK LOOPS.

IN 10-LB. BOXES.

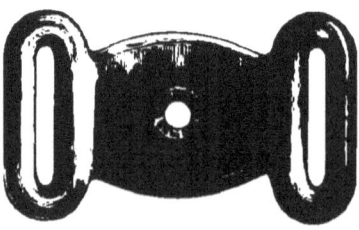

⅞, 1, 1¼, 1½, 1¾ inches.

POLE CRABS.

Nos. 1 and 2.   1¼, 1⅜, 1½, 1⅝ inch.

No. 1 .... 3¼ inch Plate.
" 2 7   "

SWINGLETREE CLIP.   SWINGLETREE STAPLE.

   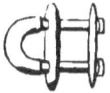

No. 1 .... 1¼ inch.   No. 1, for Swingletrees 1¼ to 2¼ inches.
" 2 .... 1½ "   " 2, "   "   2¼ to 3¼   "
                                         Finishing, 5 cents each.

FOOT-BOARD HANDLE.   RING COCK EYE.   POLE STOP.

PLOUGH CLEVICES.

Finishing, 4 cents each.

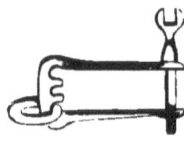

No. 1.

2½,   2¾,
2¾ lbs.   3 lbs.

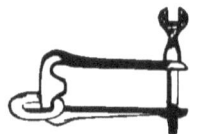

No. 2.

2½,   3 inches.
3½ lbs.   3½ lbs.

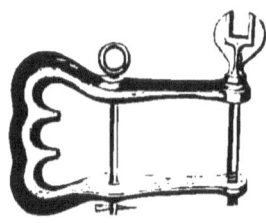

No. 20.

2 inches, 1½ lbs.

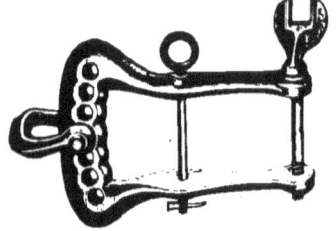

Nos. 30 and 40.

No. 30, 2½ inches .... 2½ lbs.
" 40, 2½ " .... 3¾ lbs.

No. 0, ¾ inch.

SHAW'S PATENT FERRULES.

Patented December 10th, 1867.

IN 10-LB. BOXES.

Narrow, for Handles.

½,   ⅝,   ¾,   ⅞,   1 inch.

15 cents per lb.

Wide, for Swingletrees.

⅝,   ¾,   1,   1¼,   1⅜,   1½,   1¾ inches.

12 cents per lb.

YOKE TIPS.

" ½, 1 inch.
15 cents per lb.

SWINGLETREE TIPS.

No. 1.

No. 2.

No. 3.

" 1 inch.
15 cents per lb.

SHAFT TIPS.

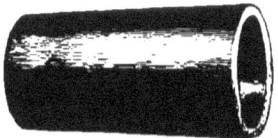

⅞ 1 inch,—15 cents per lb.

POLE TIPS.

1, 1⅛, 1¼, 1⅜, 1½ inches.
15 cents per lb.

POLE CRABS.

Nos. 3 and 4.

No. 3—1¼ inches.   No. 4—1½ inches.
15 cents per lb.

HAME LOOPS.

1 inch.. 12 cents per lb.

CHAIN T's.

Nos. 1, 2, 3
3¼, 3½, 4¼ inches.

No. 4—3¼ inches. 12 cents per lb.

TRACE CLIPS.

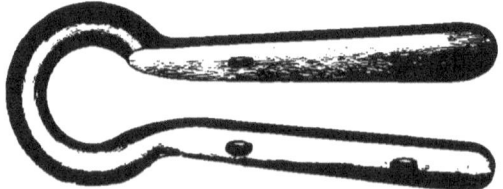

12 cents per lb.

HAME RINGS.

No. 1 — 1 inch, Light
 " 2 — 1" " Heavy
 3 — 1 " "
12 cents per lb.

HAME STAPLES.

12 cents per lb.

HAME HOOKS.

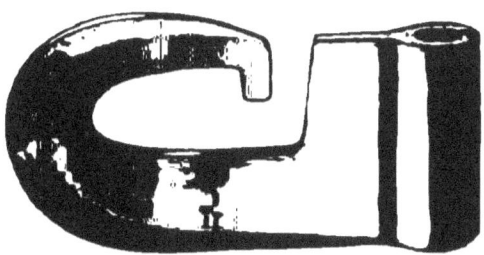

12 cents per lb.

CHAIN SWIVELS.

Nos. 0, 1, 1 2

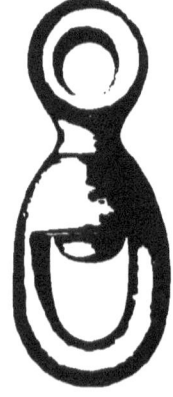  

Nos. 5. 10. 20.

CHAIN SWIVELS.

No. 4.

No. 7, 4 inches.

No. 8.
Style of Nos. 6, 8 and 9.
No. 6, 2 inches.   No. 8, 4 inches.
No. 9, 4½ inches.   15 cents per lb.

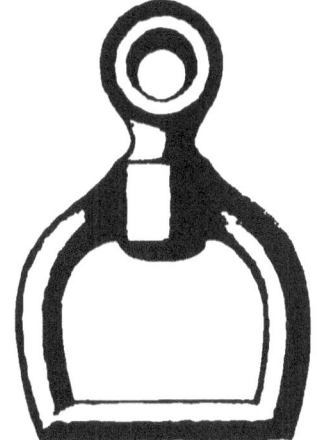

No. 5.
Style of Nos. 5 and 7.
No. 5, 4 inches.   No. 7, 4 inches.

THUMB NUTS.

IN 10 LB. BOXES.

1, 7/8 inch.

No. 2.

20 cents per lb.

No. 4—1 inch Hole.
" *5*—1¼ "

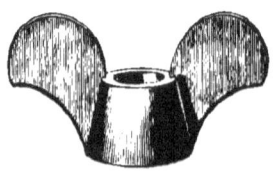

6, 1 inch.

18 cents per lb.

THUMB SCREWS.

¼ inch thick ..... ¾ inch long.
⅜ "   "   ..... ¾ and 1 inch long.
½ "   "   ..... 1 and 1¼ "   "

15 cents per lb.

SHIFTING TOP PLATES.

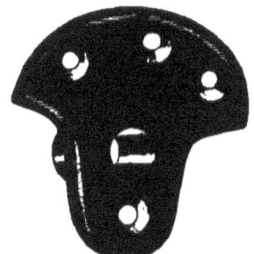

15 cents per lb.

CLINCH RINGS.
MALLEABLE IRON.

½, ⅜, ¼, ⅛ inch Hole............................ 12 cents per lb.

Malleable Iron Axle Washers,

To prevent the Linch Pin from bouncing out.

THORNLEY'S PATENT.

1,	$1\frac{1}{8}$,	$1\frac{1}{4}$,	$1\frac{3}{8}$,	$1\frac{1}{2}$,	$1\frac{5}{8}$,	$1\frac{3}{4}$,	$1\frac{7}{8}$,	2,	$2\frac{1}{8}$,	$2\frac{1}{4}$,	$2\frac{3}{8}$,	$2\frac{1}{2}$,	$2\frac{5}{8}$ inch Hole.
25,	25,	45,	60,	60,	60,	65,	65,	65,	70,	70,	70,	75,	75 cts. per Pair.

CAST-IRON WASHERS.

$\frac{3}{8}$, $\frac{1}{2}$, $\frac{5}{8}$, $\frac{3}{4}$, 1, $1\frac{1}{8}$, $1\frac{1}{4}$, $1\frac{1}{2}$ inches.. **4 cents per lb.**

SPRING SHACKLES.

1¼,	1⅜,	2,	2¼,	2½,	2¾,	3 inch.
$1 00	$1 36	$1 50	$2 00	$2 13	$2 38	$2 50

PER SET OF FOUR.

TRUNK DOVE TAILS.

MALLEABLE IRON

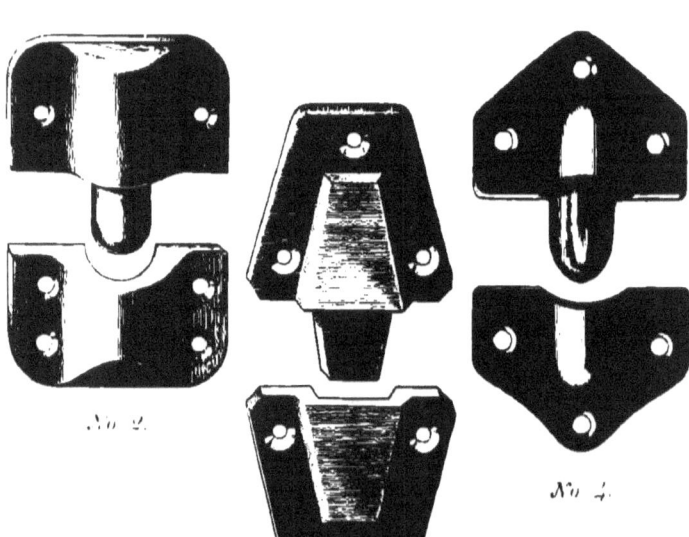

No. 2.

No. 3.

No. 4.

```
No. 2, Japanned ..............................................$4 50 per gross.
 "  3,     "    ..............................................  3 50    "
    4,     "    ..............................................  3 50    "
```

TRUNK DOVE TAILS.

MALLEABLE IRON.

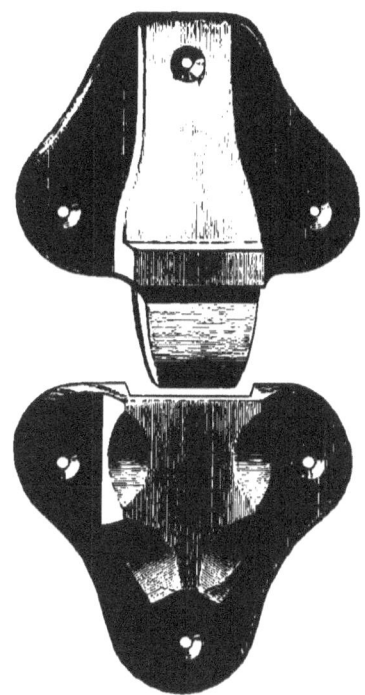

No. 1.

Japanned..$9 00 per gross.

TRUNK PLATES.

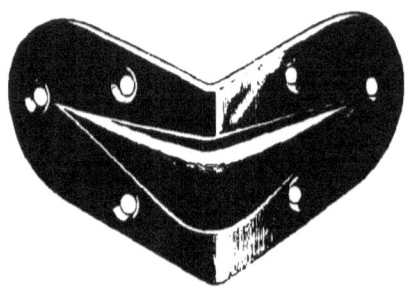

Nos. 1 and 9.

MALLEABLE IRON.

No. 1, Japanned,	1.	inch wide,	2¼ by 2¼ inches		$5 25	per gross
" 2,	"	1.	"	5½ by 2¼ "	14 50	"
" 4,	"	1½	"	1½ by 1½ "	3 00	"
" 5,	"	2	"	2½ by 2½ "	13 00	"
" 6,	"	1.	"	1½ by 1½ "	3 50	"

WROUGHT IRON.

No. 6½, Japanned,	1¼	inch wide,	1¼ by 1¼ inch		$1 50	per gross.
" 7,	"	1¼	"	1½ by 1½ "	1 75	"
" 8,	"	1.	"	1½ by 1½ "	1 85	"
" 9,	"	1½	"	2 by 2 "	2 25	"

TRUNK PLATES.

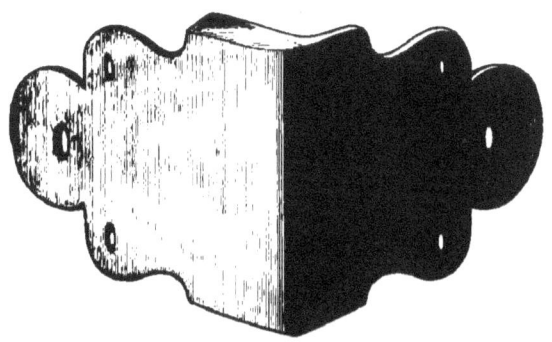

No. 12.

No. 12—Japanned, 2 inches wide, 2¼ by 2¼ inches..................$7 00 per gross.

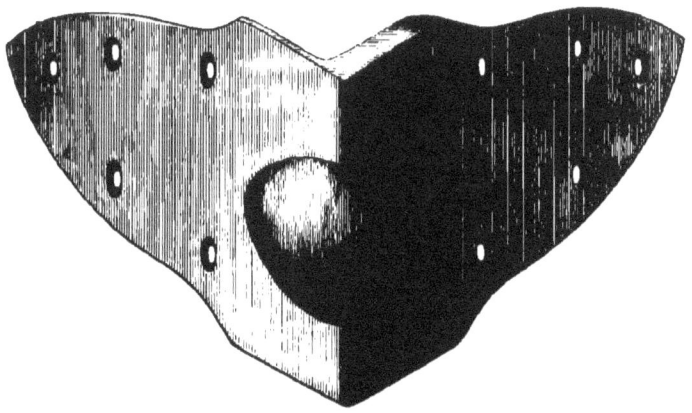

No. 13.

No. 13—Japanned, 2½ inches wide, 3½ by 3½ inches..................$11 00 per gross.

TRUNK PLATES.

MALLEABLE IRON.

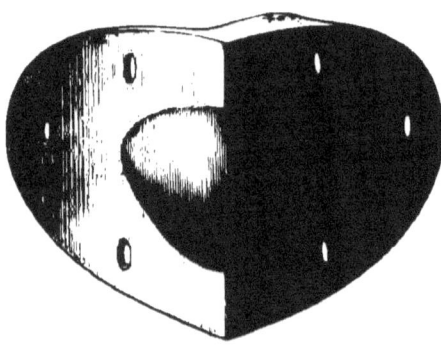

No. 3—Japanned, 2½ inches wide—2½ by 2½ inches .... $9.25 per gross.

TRUNK ROLLERS.

No. 0.

No. 10.

No. 0, 65 gross in a barrel .... $1.56 per gross.
" 10, 60 " " " .... 1.90 "

TRUNK ROLLERS.

No. 2.

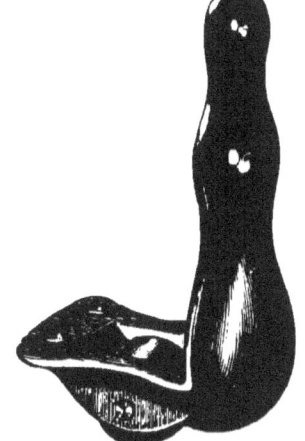

No. 1.

No. 2.

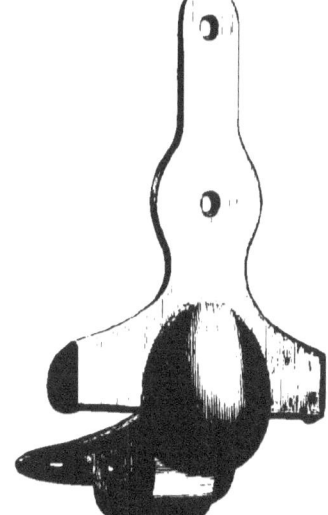

No. 3.

		JAPANNED.	TINNED.
No 1,	22 gross in a barrel	$5 40	$8 00 per gross.
" 2,	16 " " "	6 50	10 25 "
" 3,	12 " " "	7 20	11 00 "
" 4,	30 " " "	4 30	6 50 "

Wrought Iron Trunk Hinges.

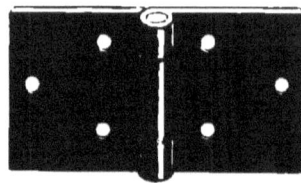

1 inch............................15 gross in a keg..............................$1 75 per gross pairs
1¼ " ....10 "   "   " .... 2 25 "   "   "

6 inches by 1¼ inch...............4 gross in a keg ....$6 00 per gross pairs
7 " by 1¼ " ....3 "   "   " .... 7 00 "   "   "

TRUNK HANDLE CAPS

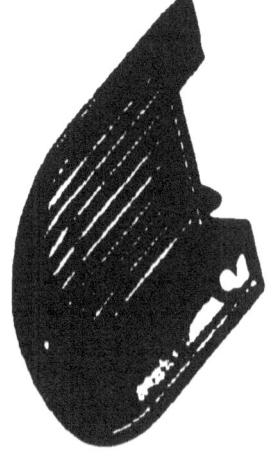

TRUNK BUTTONS.

1¼ inch, Japanned .... $0 30 per gross.
1½   "   "   0 36   "

TRUNK HANDLE LOOPS.

1⅜ inch, Japanned $4 00 per gross

SATCHEL PLATES.

Japanned................   .... $1 75 per gross

SAUCE-PAN HANDLES.

MALLEABLE IRON

5, 6 7 inches.   8, 9, 10 inches.

	JAPANNED.	TINNED.
5 inches	$2 25	$2 80 per gross.
6 "	3 25	4 10 "
7 "	3 75	4 70 "
8 "	5 50	6 90 "
9 "	6 75	8 40 "
10 "	7 50	9 30 "

DAMPER HANDLES.

Japanned	$7 00 per gross.
Tinned	10 00 " "

LID KNOBS.

No. 100.   *No. 190.*

No. 100—Japanned	$0 40 per gross.
" 190— "	0 50 "

Wrought-Iron Kettle Ears.

TINNED.

 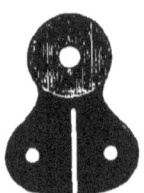 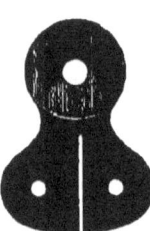 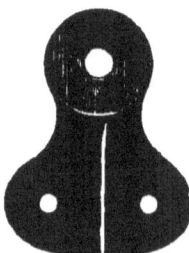

No. 1. *No. 2.* *No. 3.* *No. 4.*

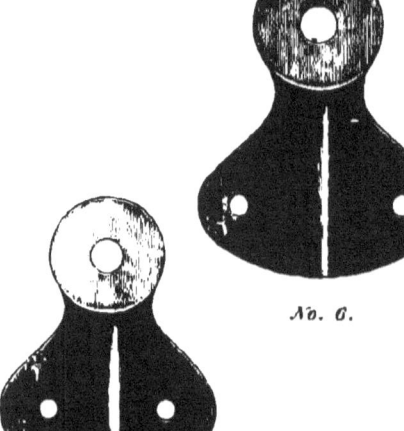

No. 6.

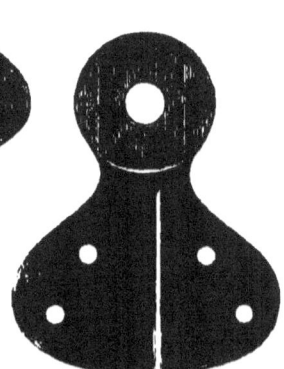

No. 5. *No. 7.*

No.		
1	$1 20	per gross pairs.
2	1 30	" " "
3	1 60	" " "
4	2 10	" " "
5	2 30	" " "
6	2 60	" " "
7	3 25	" " "

Malleable-Iron Kettle Ears.

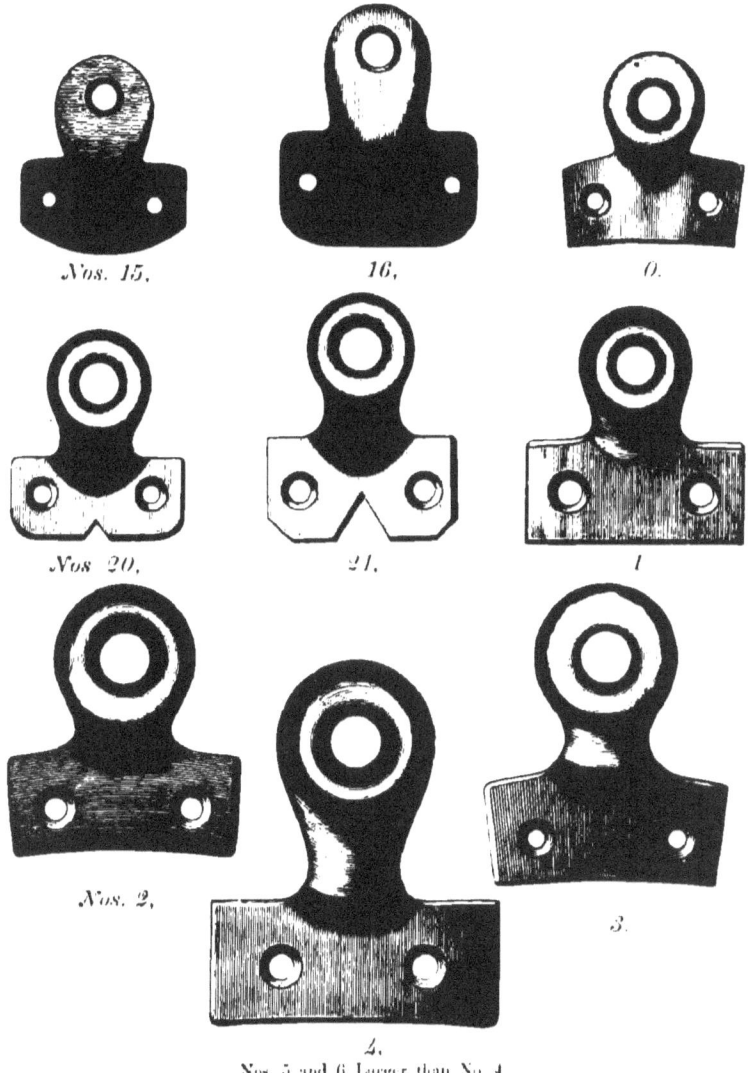

Nos. 15, 16, 0.
Nos 20, 21, 1
Nos. 2, 3.
4.
Nos. 5 and 6 Larger than No. 4.

Nos. 15 and 16, Tinned .... 17 cents per lb.
All other Nos., " .... .15 "
 "   "   not " .... .10 "

Coal Hod Handles and Ears.

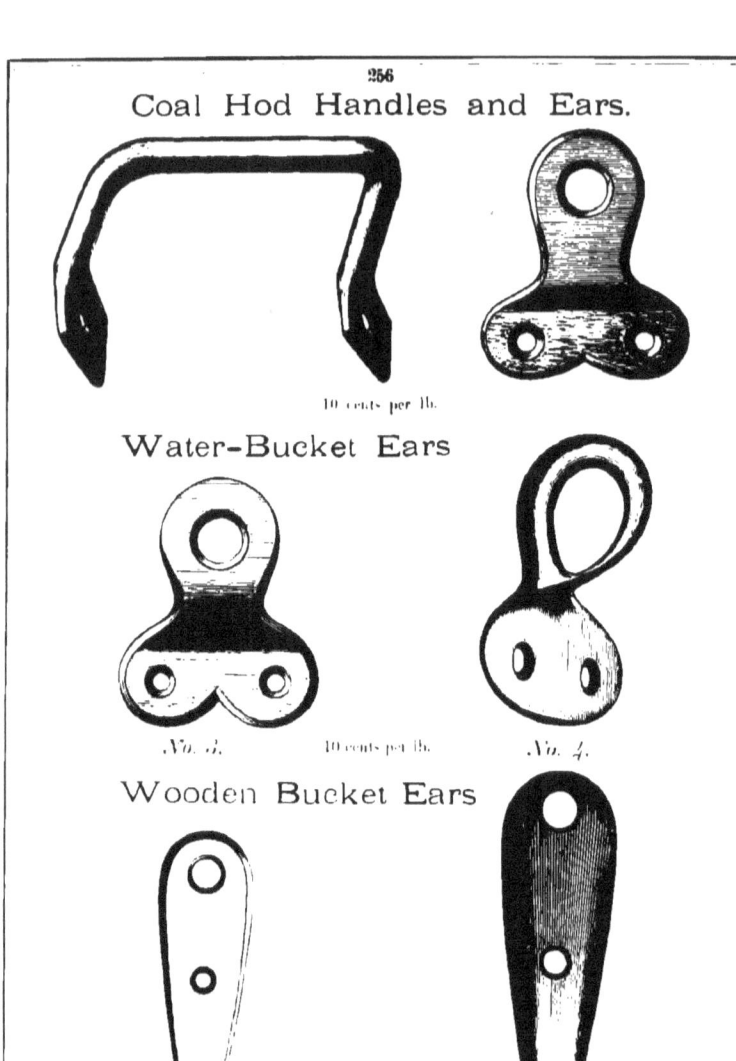

10 cents per lb.

Water-Bucket Ears

No. 3.   10 cents per lb.   No. 4.

Wooden Bucket Ears

No. 1.   No. 2.

Tinned ....15 cents per lb.
Not "   ....10 "

DISH-PAN HANDLES.

MALLEABLE IRON.

No. 1.

No. 2.

Tinned ....15 cents per lb.

STOVE-PIPE DAMPERS.

With Malleable-Iron Rods and Nuts.

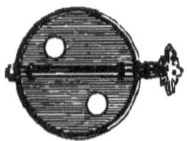

$1 00	$1 12	$1 25	$1 45	$1 60	$2 00	$2 80	$4 00 per dozen.
4	4½	5	5½	6	6½	7	8 inches.

COAL SHOVELS.

Cast-Iron, with or without Holes............ ....$15 00 per gross.

ROOFING GROOVERS.

No 1, ¾ by 1 inch..... ....$10 00 per dozen
" 2, 1 by 1¼ " .... 10 50 "

MILK-CAN HANDLE HOLDERS.

Malleable Iron, Tinned ..... 15 cents per lb.

MILK-CAN HANDLES.

Full Size Cut of No. 1.   No. 2 Larger than No. 1.

Grey Iron ..... 5 cents per lb.
" Tinned ..... 10 " "
Malleable Iron, " ..... 15 " "

STOVE KNOBS.

No. 3.
8 cents per lb.

GREY IRON HANDLES.
For Water Coolers, Toilet Ware, &c.

Nos. 2,   *3,*   *5,*

7 cents per lb.

LID HANDLES.

No. 3.
Grey Iron, with Wrought Pins..8 cts. per lb.

Wall Nails.   Floor Nails.

12 cents per lb.   *Nos 1, 2.*
                        12 cents per lb.
                        No. 1, Brass, 50 " "

Malleable-Iron Handles.

FOR WATER-COOLERS, TOILET WARE, &c.

Nos. 1,   *4,*   *5.*

Tinned ....15 cents per lb.
Not "   ....10 "   "

LID HANDLES—Malleable Iron.

No. 1.

Tinned ....15 cents per lb.

TUREEN FEET—Malleable Iron.

Nos. 1, 2 and 3.

Tinned ....15 cents per lb.

262
STOVE TURNBUCKLES.

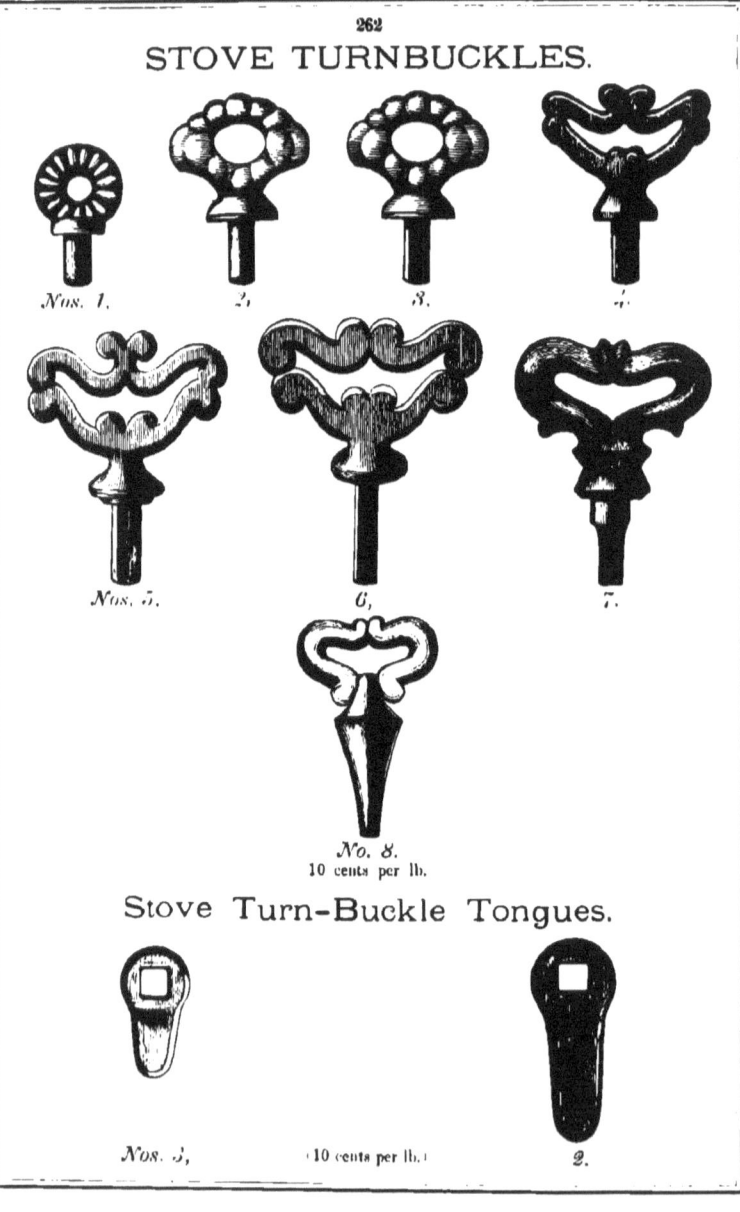

Nos. 1.   2.   3.   4.

Nos. 5.   6.   7.

No. 8.
10 cents per lb.

Stove Turn-Buckle Tongues.

Nos. 1,   10 cents per lb.   2.

STOVE-LATCH CATCHES.

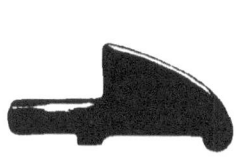

No. 1.   *No. 4.*

10 cents per lb.

STOVE HINGE PINS.

No. 1.   *No. 2.*

10 cents per lb.

STOVE LATCHES.

4½, 5, 5½, 6, 7, 8, 9 inches .... 10 cents per lb.

Hydrant Handles and Stays.

10 cents per lb.

Wash-Pave Keys.   Gas Wrenches.

⅛ and ⁷⁄₁₆ inches.

   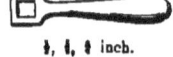

⅜, ½, ⅝ inch.

½ by 1 inch.
1 by 1½ "

12 cents per lb.   8 cents per lb.

Gas Keys.   Floor Plates.

8 cents per lb.   10 cents per lb.

www.ingramcontent.com/pod-product-compliance
Lightning Source LLC
Chambersburg PA
CBHW032109230426
43672CB00009B/1682